Building a Pentium Server

by Nate Vanderschaaf

Abacus

Copyright © 1999   Abacus Software Inc.
                          5370 52nd Street SE
                          Grand Rapids, MI 49512
                          www.abacuspub.com

Printed in the United States of America

ISBN 1-55755-328-9

10 9 8 7 6 5 4 3 2 1

Contents

Chapter 3:
The Component Hardware of a Typical Server 17

Chapter 4:
Assembling the Server 55

Chapter 5:
Installing Windows NT Server 143

Introduction

Why build your own server?

As companies grow from mom-and-pop shops to small businesses, their data becomes more critical. You too, have grown with this company. Somewhere along the line, by declaration or by default, you took charge of IT: Information Technology. Lately, your data has become more difficult to manage. You realize that the PCs around the office need to work together. You want to send e-mail to each other and to the outside world. You'd like Web access for your employees and a Web page for your company. You also need a central place to keep your files. One big, fast printer for everyone would also be nice. Your company needs a server computer.

Now you know you need a server, but aren't sure what should be inside it. Choosing a home PC was easy. Just talk to the teenage salesperson, pay about $2,000 and take it home. Does it matter which one you get? All the PCs are pretty much the same anyway. You took it home, and it worked great right out of the box. If everything wasn't exactly what you needed, it wasn't a big deal. If it broke down, you could take it in and wait a few days for the repair; and besides, everyone else seemed to know tons about computers and enjoyed troubleshooting with you.

But everything changes with a business server. Now, it's the company's money, and servers can cost up to $20,000 each. That's a lot of money to spend, and you want to do it right. You could talk to a well-dressed salesman in a suit, pay about $20,000 and have the servers delivered to the office. But there's a better way—build your own.

This book addresses lots of questions:

▲ Does it matter what kind you get? Aren't all servers pretty much the same?

▲ Won't it work right out of the box?

▲ If it isn't exactly what I need, it will be close enough, won't it?

▲ Is it upgradable?

▲ If it breaks down, can't I just get it fixed?

▲ Did I pay too much?

This book will show you how to build a server that's as good as or better than a Compaq, a Hewlett-Packard, an IBM or a Dell, for less money. Picking and choosing your high-quality, name-brand components, you can save money by buying only the components you need, while keeping a future upgrade in mind. The corporate manufacturers don't want you to upgrade! They want to sell you another overpriced server in a year or two! If you follow the guidelines in this book, there are no disadvantages to building your own server. So read on! Learn to build your own Pentium II server, and save yourself future headaches, downtime, and most of all, money!

This book will show you how to build a server to maximize the major concerns that are unique to servers:

▲ **Speed**—It's not a luxury, it's a necessity.

▲ **Uptime**—It must be reliable. A business can't afford not being able to reach payroll accounts, customer databases or other important data.

▲ **Scalability**—You're not going to want to build or buy a new computer one year from now. Considering scalability now will make upgrading and/or expanding your network much easier and cheaper.

This book will explain all of the concepts in plain English and allow you to build a server ready for just about any server need, including:

▲ File servers

▲ Proxy servers

▲ Application servers

▲ Enterprise servers (manage users and resources)

▲ Web servers

▲ FTP servers

▲ Process servers

▲ Intranet servers

▲ Internet servers

▲ CD-ROM servers

▲ E-mail servers

▲ Voice-mail servers

▲ Real-time video delivery servers

We'll build a server ready to run Windows NT, Novell NetWare or UNIX.

This book is not designed to teach Windows NT Administration. Having said that, it is an excellent resource for hardware reference. I wrote this book to teach anyone who has minimal computer knowledge how to build a Pentium II Microsoft Windows NT server. There are many references to Windows NT terms in this book. This book will teach you to install and configure the hardware for Windows NT. If you are new to Windows NT, you need to learn Windows NT Administration from a different source. After you are done with this book, consider beginning a course of study in Windows NT Administration.

This book will introduce you to networking, but assumes some knowledge of PC hardware. If you are new to PC hardware, we highly recommend that you read *Building Your Own PC* as an introduction to this book.

Chapter 1:
Introduction to Networking

Definition

Networking is connecting multiple computers so that their users may interact, share an electronic workload and communicate more effectively.

History

Networking arose out of necessity. All current networking technology is based on the Internet, which the US government created to ensure nation-wide communication if the phone system failed due to natural or man-made disasters. The first computers connected to the Net were very powerful, and the connections were plenty fast for their day (the late '60s). The Internet primarily uses UNIX computers, with the TCP/IP protocol.

Special Note

UNIX is a very powerful operating system for all kinds of computers, not just PCs. However, you can try UNIX, and you don't even have to pay. Visit www.linux.org for more information about a very powerful version of UNIX designed for PCs. I recommend Red Hat 5 if you are new to linux, although Debian 2.0 is the best! Remember, the world is not all Microsoft!

Then a company called Novell came along in the 'eighties. Novell realized a vision of medium-scale networking for the future by inventing NetWare and the IPX/SPX protocol, which grew very popular. Also in the 'eighties, Bob Metcalfe (the founder of 3Com) invented Ethernet, the network card technology used today in almost all computers. Microsoft eventually joined the game with their networking protocol, NetBeui, designed for small-scale networks. NetBeui is extremely limited and is proprietary. Worst of all, it can't be used for Wide Area Networks (WANs).

Computer networking still wasn't a household term, but that was about to change. With the advent of the World Wide Web, office personnel and home users saw the need to connect to the Internet. The TCP/IP protocol soon became available for all platforms, not just UNIX. Windows NT 5.0 will ship with TCP/IP standard instead of NetBeui, and Novell NetWare 5.0 can use TCP/IP natively, no longer requiring the presence of IPX/SPX. TCP/IP has emerged as the networking protocol of choice.

Why do you need a network? You need a network if:

- ❖ You have more than one PC in your office. In fact, you may have dozens or hundreds.

- ❖ You don't want to buy a separate copy of each software program for every machine. (It's illegal to buy one copy and install it on all the individual computers).

- ❖ You want to send e-mail to each other, the Internet or other offices.

- ❖ You want to share a printer.

- ❖ You want to share files, hard drive space or a removable media drive, like a tape drive or other drive.

Physical Layouts of Computer Networks

Bus

All other layouts are variants of this basic concept. A bus layout looks like this:

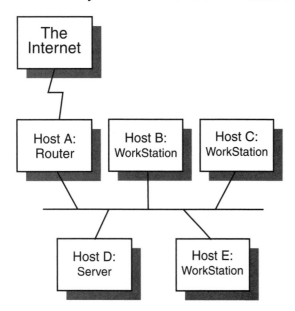

Each intelligent device is called a *host*, including workstations, routers, switches and servers. Each host has access to the bus, and when it wants to talk to another host, it listens to the bus. If no one else is talking, it talks and everyone else listens. The appropriate host then responds, and other hosts will have a chance to communicate later. Be aware that only two hosts can use the bus at once. For example, if host A is talking to host B, host C cannot communicate with host D, because a host uses the entire bus to communicate. This is true for all layouts.

The bus layout is the most basic configuration. A computer's bus is named after a city or school bus route, and it serves the same purpose. The term *bus* applies to any medium of communication for a computer or network. There are several busses inside a computer, and usually only one or two outside (the network).

Star

This is really the same as bus, described above, with each user connected to a central point. Sometimes referred to as "collapsed backbone," this system has several advantages. The central location makes it easy to manage. And if someone accidentally kicks a cable loose under his desk, *e.g.*, he only disconnects himself—everyone else remains on the network. Understand that neither configuration is faster; star is just easier to manage and has fewer problems in the real world. Remember from before, the network is still just one shared bus: if host A is talking to host B, host C can't communicate with host D.

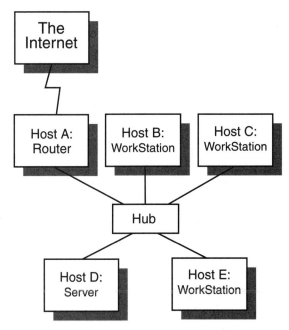

Ring

This is a modification of bus. Just connect the ends of the bus together with the computers connected in a ring. This ring contains a special message called a *token*, which a host must possess before it may speak (sort of like the conch from *Lord of the Flies*). When a host receives the token, the host can talk with another host, but after a set amount of time it must pass the token to the next host. If a host doesn't have anything to say, it immediately passes the token to the next host.

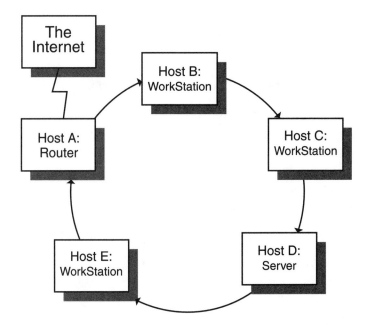

Tree

This type of network is very difficult to use for computers. It works best for one-way systems, like cable TV. Because the network is laid out in a tree structure, an entire city or half of a state might have to be rewired in a star or hybrid configuration to avoid data bottlenecks.

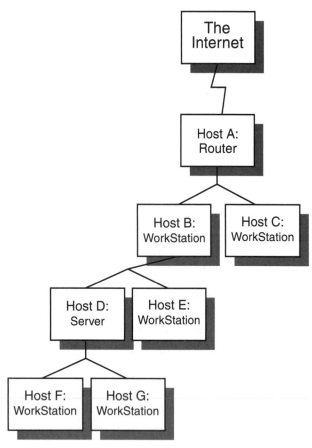

Multiple connections (Hybrid structure or Multi-homed system)

In a hybrid or multi-homed configuration, a host simply connects to one or more of its nearest neighbors and can reach the other computers through these neighbors. The Internet is an example of this kind of network. You are probably used to being connected to the Internet at only one place, like your home computer. Your home computer with a modem is one leaf on a tree-structured network formed by your Internet Service Provider (ISP). The ISP then connects to the next nearest Internet site, and so on. Keep in mind that no one "King Daddy Internet Server" exists at the top of the network, but rather thousands of loosely associated computers all connect through one another.

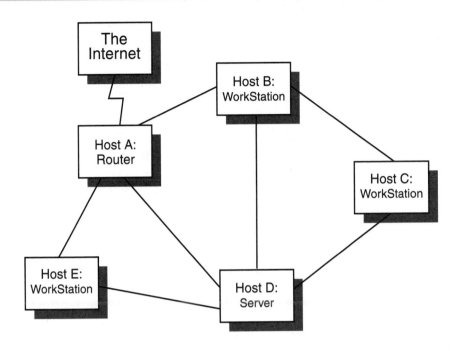

Networking Hardware

Modems

A modem is like an Ethernet card, but it operates much more slowly. Fast Ethernet (transferring 100 million bits per second) is almost 2,000 times faster than a 56K modem (which transmits 56 thousand bits per second). Modems are not for permanent connections; they open a dedicated channel to another modem in a server, and that server then passes messages via a network card.

Network Cards

These are the adapter cards that go into a slot in a server, a workstation, a printer and other devices. Network cards are cheap and easy to use (a quality Ethernet / Fast Ethernet card costs less than $100).

Ethernet cards use a strange type of communication. It's called CSMA/CD (Carrier Sense Multiple Access with Collision Detect). Here's how it works: The cards are all trying to talk to each other at the same time. Understand that while one card talks to another card, all cards must listen. It doesn't matter how long the wires are, how many hubs are in between or how many computers are on the network. What matters is whether there is a silent moment for a card to begin talking to another card. All cards are always listening (when they are not talking). Every now and then, two cards will talk at the same time, resulting in a *collision*. This happens just like it does at a large dinner party. If two people talk simultaneously, they both shut up for a moment, then try again. Eventually, one will go first and the other waits for a break in the conversation.

Hubs

A hub is a place to plug in a bunch of network cards. In terms of useful networking work, a hub does absolutely nothing. The hub merely replicates signals that appear on any port to the other ports. The hub doesn't even know that the electrical impulses are data! Hubs don't require a server; they are stand-alone devices (although they don't serve any purpose unless something is plugged into them). Hubs are cheap, costing less than $100 for an eight-port Ethernet hub. Hubs are only needed in a star configuration:

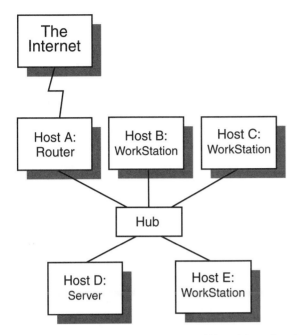

You need to connect the hubs like this. The device at the center is the hub and looks like this up close:

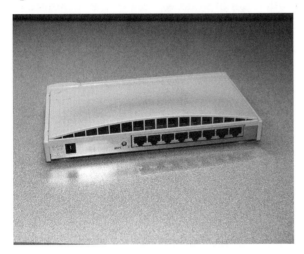

The outlets on this device are called *ports*, and each one accepts one connection.

Be sure to get a 10/100 auto-sensing PCI Ethernet network card with an RJ-45 (sometimes called "10-base-T") connector. Be careful: this connector will accept an RJ-11 phone plug, but don't plug a phone cord into a hub or a network card. Buy Ethernet cables from a mail order facility like DataComm Warehouse (www.warehouse.com) or your local store. Be sure they are rated for category five (CAT 5). The connector is the same on both ends and looks like this:

RJ-45 Jack up close

It doesn't make any difference which ports on the hub are plugged into which computers. The only reason ports are numbered is that it is easier to determine who is plugged in where by the activity light on the hub, especially when the cable is too tangled, is built into the wall or otherwise can't be traced by hand.

Hubless Connection

Two network cards can be hooked together without the hub in between. For this, you need a piece of crossover cable or a crossover coupler; the important wires are reversed for this special purpose. Order one or have one custom built for you. Mine is a three-inch cable with a standard coupler:

Multiple Hubs

Two hubs can be hooked together to increase the number of hub ports. Again, use a crossover cable or crossover coupler. The other option is using a special uplink port on the hub. Many hubs have a dedicated uplink port or a little selector switch labeled like this:

Use this port to connect another hub. Connect the uplink port to a regular port on the other hub; don't connect the two uplink ports together and don't use a crossover cable. Some hubs are "five-port hubs" that actually contain six ports. You can connect port six to port one, two, three, four or five on another five-port hub.

If your server is plenty fast and there are still performance problems on the network, the network can be segmented using switches and routers. Don't uplink hubs unless you have to. Two five-port uplinked hubs (yielding eight usable ports) work together well, but they can cause more collisions (and be slower) than one eight port hub. (Two hubs can work as one by *stacking*, but two stackable hubs cost about the same as one that's twice the size).

Up to four Ethernet hubs can be connected between hosts. Each cable must not be longer than 100 meters. If you're working with Fast Ethernet, however, you may only directly connect two hubs. The total cable length between hosts in this case can not exceed 205 meters, and each cable must not be longer than 100 meters (the cable connecting the two hubs should be five meters or shorter).

Switches

A switch is just like a hub, but it doesn't replicate signals to all the ports. It only replicates the signals to the port that needs it! So, why would anyone use a hub instead of a switch? You guessed it! Switches are expensive (about $800 for a 12-port Ethernet switch). So, why would anyone use a switch instead of a hub? Just as you eventually need more than one phone line in your office, eventually you need more than one segment in your network.

Routers

A router is a special kind of server that connects two or more networks. This is useful when a network has so many computers on it that switches are too slow to separate the traffic. Nothing is bigger or faster than a router. A PC with a modem and a network card can be a router, but a dedicated hardware router is faster.

Workstation (Client)

This describes everybody on the network who needs to be serviced (and protected). There is a limit to how many computers you can put on a network. This is an inexact science, and it has evolved into an art form! The number of computers that can successfully function on a network depends on three things: The software that's running (games like Quake2 use a lot of the network *bandwidth*), the number of people actually using the network, and most importantly, **the speed of the servers being accessed!** With all of the workstations accessing the same place, the server is the bottleneck! *A fast server is essential for a fast network.*

Servers

Servers have a dedicated existence "to protect and to serve." They are both the servant and the policeman for the network. But what makes a computer a "server," instead of a "workstation" or just a "PC"? The only difference between a server and a normal PC is that a server performs some functions for other computers on the network. If a computer has this much responsibility, it had better be good at what it does. We'll show you how to build it.

Next, we'll look at some different types of servers.

Chapter 2:
Different Types of Servers

N ext, let's look at some different types of servers. Odds are, your idea of what your server should do will fit one of these descriptions.

Intranet Servers

File Server

A file server shares files with users. For example, if you have a budget in an Excel spreadsheet, you can store the spreadsheet file on the server and make it available to anyone on the network. The file server can prevent two users from modifying the spreadsheet at the same time. Storing the file on the network also allows it to be backed up for retrieval, in case the hard drive fails.

Print Server

A print server establishes print queues, manages print jobs, and determines who can print to which printers. Many file servers also handle this function.

Application Server

This server's sole purpose is to control who runs a program on his or her local machine. If you only own five copies of Microsoft Word, but you have 10 computers and you want all 10 of them to be able to run Microsoft Word, you can install Word on the application server. When a user double-clicks the icon on his computer, the application is loaded from the server's hard drive into the memory of the user's workstation. The server will only allow five computers to run Word at the same time, but usually not everyone will want to use it at once, and maybe eight copies will suffice so that almost no one is ever unable run Word. This becomes more useful when you want to run software that is extremely expensive or is almost never used. 3-D Studio Max, *e.g.*, costs $3,000 per copy. You could buy one copy, and if it is rarely used, make it available to 10 users, for a cost savings of $27,000.

As applications have grown larger, launching one from a server has gotten slower. A modified form of application serving, called *certificate control*, combats this. AutoCAD and PhotoShop use certificate control, for example. It works like this: You buy five copies of the program and install it on 10 computers. When a user launches the program, it contacts the application server to obtain a certificate, and the program will run. Once five users have obtained certificates, the sixth user will be informed that they must wait for a certificate to become available. Certificate control is a new development, and the software company must implement it. Everyone is waiting for a standard certificate system that will control any application, but for now, those applications without certificate control must be run from the server.

Process Server

This special server can run a program that the user launches on the server. Application servers load the program onto the client computer that launched it. Process servers actually run the program themselves at the request of the user. The user only sees the interface to the program (if there is one). This is the ultimate in servers, meaning that a slower, cheaper network with slower, cheaper workstations can perform as well as a fast, expensive network with fast, expensive workstations. Unfortunately, Windows NT and Novell NetWare are not able to do this. This is only possible when running UNIX.

Proxy Server

This is a special kind of Internet server that gets on the Internet instead of a workstation to retrieve the Web pages or files. The information is then passed to the workstation (or other server) across the LAN. Proxy servers are useful because they provide security (you can control who gets in or out). They were invented because the Internet was running out of IP addresses. Two ranges of addresses were set aside for internal use on intranets; a proxy server will have an external "real" IP address and an internal "fake" IP address. Every company that has a network can use the reserved IP addresses freely and can use a proxy server to connect the computers to the Internet. A proxy server, when properly implemented, provides near seamless Internet connectivity for workstations on the inside.

Domain Controller, Domain Name Server

This server resolves the network requests by names into the network requests by numbers. For example, calvin.edu is a domain name whose IP address is 153.106.1.1. No computer can talk to ursa.calvin.edu without knowing the number 153.106.1.1. Also, the numbers and names change, and one server or workstation can't know all of them. A *domain controller* is a Windows NT term. It behaves like an Internet domain, but anyone can name it whatever he or she wants. Larry, Curly and Moe can be three computers in a domain named "Stooge." (Interesting aside: Larry, Curly and Moe are the most common names of servers in US businesses!)

Primary and Backup Domain Controllers

In a Windows NT multi-server environment, one of them ultimately controls the domain. It's good to have a back-up in case the main server goes down. If you have 10 servers and 100 workstations in a domain with only one domain controller, no one can network with anyone else if the domain controller goes down.

Internet Servers

Web (HTML, HTTP) server

The Web seems to be where all the hype is, but not many people are making money or accomplishing work on the Web. (What people really need more often than not is an FTP server, a special type of file server.) Your Web server can vary in power. It can hold a plain page with just a phone number and address or it can be more useful. You could post press releases, tech support, user manuals, hours, schedules, and product information on your Web server. However, the best kind of Web server actually does something useful, like take orders automatically. Land's End has a Web server that lets you place orders right on the Web page, using encryption to secure credit card information.

FTP (File Transfer Protocol) server

This type of server was invented before Web servers, and the Web operates in a similar manner. FTP is very plain, but like all good things, it works well. Netscape Navigator can easily view an FTP server's contents just like a Web site, and a user can easily download files. FTP servers are useful for anyone who wants to make files available on the Internet, and downloading a file via FTP is usually faster than with HTTP. You can even set up links to FTP inside a Web page, and the user will never even know they are using an FTP site!

E-mail server (Groupware server)

This type of server sends e-mail in, out or around an office, or to anywhere on the Internet. This is one of the most useful servers a company can have.

Now that you know what kinds of servers will suit you, let's move on and pick out the parts we'll need to build one.

Chapter 3:
The Component Hardware of a Typical Server

N|ow we need to collect the parts for our server. Along with detailed descriptions of the hardware components, you'll also find integration details and advice throughout this chapter. Pay attention to the details for a successful build.

The Microsoft Windows NT Hardware Compatibility List

All the hardware for our server should be on the Microsoft Windows NT Hardware Compatibility List, which comes in book format with Microsoft Windows NT. (The whole list of drivers, including updates, can be accessed at http://www.microsoft.com/hwtest/ (click the "Hardware Compatibility List" link). This list contains almost every piece of hardware that works with Windows NT.

This isn't just a sales pitch or licensing deal—NT is Microsoft's first true protected-mode compatible operating system. The protected modes are special modes of the processor (in our case, the Pentium II). Without protected-mode operation, any program that has a bug in it and accidentally changes a portion of RAM that contains the operating system would cause the computer to crash! But when the CPU is in protected mode, program bugs can only affect themselves. However, drivers are programs too, and some of them don't run in a protected mode! For example, video drivers under Windows NT are operated at Intel's "Ring Zero," which means they can do whatever they want. If an NT video driver has a bug in it, it can crash the computer!

Microsoft tests and approves (and sometimes writes) drivers for use under NT. The hardware supported by these drivers is listed on the hardware compatibility list. Simple, right? *Always use NT approved hardware to maximize the stability of your server.* Notice that some motherboards are listed with the systems. If you can't find the motherboard you want, just be sure to buy a motherboard with an Intel chipset, and Microsoft-approved drivers will be available for it. This rule can be extended to all parts; if it's a well-known brand of premium quality, it will most likely be approved for Windows NT. Look for the "Designed for Microsoft Windows NT" logo on retail packaging.

Here is the hardware you'll need to build and network your server computer.

The case

Besides the size, cases have two important "type" characteristics. (The size choice is easy: BIG!) The two ways to describe the type are *profile* and *form-factor*.

Profile

The Profile of the case is its general shape. After choosing a profile, we must still choose the form factor.

Common server profiles are tower, double-wide tower, and rack mount.

Tower

A tower case looks like a big PC. Tower servers are just large versions of tower computers (about 36 inches tall, 8 inches wide). Tower servers can be placed on a shelf that's mounted to a standard rack inside a cabinet, but they don't fit neatly and take up lots of space. However, they are easier to move and can be installed stand-alone in a separate room.

Double-Wide

A double-wide case looks like two tower cases glued together at the sides. These are frequently mounted on casters.

Rack-Mount

A rack-mount case is normally 19 inches wide and includes mounting brackets for industry-standard racks. Rack-mount servers are very handy, because they fit into an industry standard 19" or 24" rack inside a cabinet. The cabinet can be locked, so no one will mess with the server. Also, several rack mount servers can fit in one cabinet, and this saves space. Space inside a server room is at a premium, since a server room is frequently climate-controlled and has a fire-suppression system. Rack-mount cases are available in form-factor compatible styles.

Form-Factor

Form-factor dictates the physical case layout, the motherboard layout, and the power supply connector.

AT

This is the original case layout, from the days of the IBM AT in the '80s. A modified version, Baby AT, is smaller than the original. Baby AT motherboards will fit into an AT case, but a regular AT motherboard may not fit into a Baby AT case.

ATX

This is the most drastic change to the PC's basic configuration in a long time. ATX defined a new power supply, with "soft" power on/off capabilities, and a different connector and wiring scheme. An ATX motherboard has a corresponding power supply connector, Advanced Power

Management capabilities, and mounts in an ATX case. ATX also defines a large rectangular opening on the back of the case in which motherboard manufacturers are free to place whatever external connectors they wish.

The motherboard comes with a plate to fill this hole, giving the case a perfectly finished look on the back and providing just the right opening for the connectors. ATX has almost completely replaced AT as the standard for custom-built computers. Like Baby AT, there is also microATX; again, a microATX motherboard fits inside an ATX case, but an ATX board may not fit inside a microATX case. LPX and NLX are also subsets of the ATX standard and use the ATX-style power supply and connector.

LPX

This is an older form factor used for small workstations by OEMs, but it never really caught on for custom solutions. This is not a good choice for servers.

NLX

This new form factor replaces LPX, and may replace ATX on the desktop in the future. It is now being implemented by OEMs for value-priced desktops. It's not a good choice for servers, either.

WTX

WTX is a cutting-edge, brand-new form factor designed for midrange workstations. This will likely appear as a popular server form factor.

Proprietary

This defines just about anything else. Several PC manufacturers, including server manufacturers, have come up with their own layouts. With these layouts, nothing is guaranteed to be modular or interchangeable, and upgrading can be difficult or impossible. Avoid proprietary form factors at all costs. This is the reason standard form factors were established, and this is the single best reason to build your own server.

What should you choose? Pick ATX (or microATX) unless you crave a particular case or motherboard that isn't available in that form factor. Don't forget to buy a motherboard and power supply that is a compatible form-factor for your case.

Brands

Enlight: 8900, Addtronics: 7890A, SuperMicro: SC 801A, PC Power & Cooling: Professional Solid Steel Tower, Shin-G: SG-5101XC and GS-1000.

Our choice

We have chosen the Enlight 8900 (ATX) case for our server.

Our cost

$165 (without power supply)

Power

The main power supply provides and regulates the electicity for all the components of the server computer. These are also available in several form factors with varying connectors.

AT

AT-style power supplies use a different connector than the others.

ATX

The ATX-style is newer and can be used by ATX, LPX and NLX cases.

Big L

This type of power supply fits a special opening in the back of the case. The power connector can be either ATX or AT.

A Spare

To ensure that power interruptions can be worked around before they become problems, your server should also contain a spare power supply.

Standard

A standard power supply provides power for devices and the motherboard, until it conks out. When the power supply does fail, the computer shuts off immediately, and you must replace the power supply. Worse yet, a flaky power supply will intermittently fail, and may cause the server to reboot from time to time. This will frustrate you to no end, and you may even lose data!

Redundant

A redundant power supply provides power until it conks out, but just before it dies, it passes the duty of providing power to an identical circuit inside the power supply. The computer never notices the change.

Hot-swappable Redundant

Hot-swappable redundant power supplies can be exchanged without even turning the computer off. They slide out the back, and while one is being removed, the other one provides the power. **Choose a Hot-swappable redundant power supply for maximum uptime.**

Brands

Emacs (Zippy) fits several types of cases; Enlight (fits the Enlight case); SuperMicro (fits the SuperMicro Case); PC Power & Cooling (fits the PC P&C case).

Special Note: Redundant power supplies are hard to find. If you can, get it preinstalled with the case. Before buying the case or the power supply, make sure you have selected a case and a power supply that have been guaranteed by your vendor to work together. If you have difficulty, here are some URLs of vendors and manufacturers:

www.wetex.com	www.pcpowercooling.com	www.33comix.com
www.casedepot.com	www.amtrade.com	www.jinco.com
www.enlight.com.tw	www.supermicro.com	www.zippyusa.com
www.circotech.com	www.appro.com	

Our choice

We choose the Emacs Zippy RPD, dual 300 watt, hot swap, load sharing, with buzzer. Our power supply is hot-swappable redundant with an ATX power connector. You should buy whatever kind you need to match your case and motherboard.

Our cost

$139.00

Uninterruptible Power Supply/Source (UPS)

These boxes, usually external or rack-mounted near the server, provide power to the computer and monitor in the event of a power outage. They contain large batteries and can operate for varying lengths of time, from just long enough to shut down the server to long enough to keep everything alive until power can be restored. Some UPS units can even signal a diesel generator to start up (like in a hospital). For computers, a UPS simply plugs into the wall and provides standard power connectors on the back. Don't plug anything you don't need into a UPS. No laser printers, pencil sharpeners or refrigerators, and certainly no electric lights! You will barely have enough power to run your server and save your critical information, let alone chill your lunch. A UPS also conditions the power and protects things that are plugged into it from spikes, surges, brownouts, and unlike surge suppressors, gradual line voltage increases. Good UPSes come with software and a serial cable to connect to the server and to communicate with the server about the status of power, the condition of the batteries and the approximate time that the server can run during a power outage. During an outage, when only five minutes of runtime remain, the server can shut itself down to avoid file corruption from having the power abruptly cut off.

Types of UPSes

These types describe how the UPS manages power.

Standby

A standby UPS conditions the power coming in. In the event of a power failure, it turns on its internal transformer and switches to its internal batteries. This takes less than 10 milliseconds (ms), which is usually quick enough to avoid interrupting the flow to the computer's internal power supply. The computer's power supply can usually make up for this brief interruption.

In-line

An in-line UPS is always running on its batteries unless they fail. If a battery fails, the UPS switches to the wall current for the computer. It charges the batteries from the wall while simultaneously providing power to the computer and monitor. No switching is required during a power failure. These are the most expensive UPSes, and the batteries frequently need to be replaced.

Line-interactive

Line-interactive is a modified standby UPS. It operates very much like a standby UPS, but it keeps the transformer powered on all the time and can switch to the batteries much more quickly (in less than 5 ms). This is necessary for servers, because the load is so heavy on the internal power supply that it may not be able to compensate for a lack of power flow for very long.

You should also consider how you will manage the box.

Unmanaged

Unmanaged UPSes are the cheapest type available. These have no connectors but power in and power out.

Manageable

Dumb UPSes have a serial cable and sometimes come with software, but have limited features. Each one can only minimally interact with the server. The dumb UPS only shorts pins on the serial cable, and the monitoring software checks to determine whether the pins are shorted. When the software detects the status of the UPS to be "On battery," it can send an alert message in a window. When the software detects that the UPS is at "two minutes to shut down," it also sends an alert and can initiate the shutdown sequence. There is usually a delay before the shutdown sequence is initiated, in order to overcome those momentary lapses of power versus a total power failure. The shutdown sequence can be quite complex, and a friend of mine even has his servers send a text message to his pager. He isn't fond of waking up in the middle of the night, but he rests easier knowing that his beeper will immediately notify him of "No power to server: Larry, Curly and Moe shutdown initiated: will complete in five minutes."

Intelligent UPSes have a connector from the serial port to the server, and usually come with software for enhanced management. The best UPSes come with network ports so they can be managed from anywhere on the network. Intelligent UPSes can tell you how long they've been turned on, the approximate power life remaining at the current load, the health of each individual battery inside (whether or not the batteries are capable of being charged) and other useful information. Intelligent UPSes will alert a designated server or servers (if they are network manageable) instead of waiting to be asked. They also usually provide much more in-depth information.

Choose a UPS that is line-interactive and can run your server for at least 15 minutes under heavy load.

Brands

American Power Conversion (www.apcc.com), Tripp Lite (www.tripplite.com), Opti-UPS by ViewSonic (www.optiups.com), Best-Power (www.bestpower.com), P K Electronics

Our choice

We've chosen a Smart-UPS 1000, from APC. It's an intelligent, line-interactive UPS. It also has an expandability function; several additional, external battery packs can be added to the Smart-UPS 1000 in case we don't have enough run time. It also comes with PowerChute software for Windows NT.

Our cost

$500

Motherboards

We need a quality motherboard, one worthy of being in a server.

Parameters to consider:

Chipsets

These onboard chips interact with all the other parts. The chipsets are defined by Intel and sold to other manufacturers. Intel also manufactures motherboards. Currently, the 440BX, which supports up to a Pentium II 450, is the most popular. The 440GX supports the Pentium II Xeon, as well. (CPU support is also dependent upon the motherboard). The 450NX supports only the Pentium II Xeon. The 450NX/GX supports only the Pentium Pro. Don't buy the 440LX or EX! These chipsets aren't for CPUs faster than 333 MHz; you can run the slower chips on the other chipsets.

See http://developer.intel.com/design/pcisets/linecard.htm for a chart of all the current chipsets.

Form factor

This choice is easy. This has to match your case and power supply. Usually, choose ATX.

Number of processors

Choose a board that is at least dual-processor capable. You can add the second processor later.

Slots

Get as many PCI slots as you can. If you have two identical boards for the same price, but one has more PCI slots, choose the one with more PCI slots. Most boards will have an AGP slot as well. Newer motherboards also have 64-bit PCI slots, which look like a PCI slot only longer. They are compatible with PCI 32-bit cards.

On-board Options

Motherboards are available with several onboard options: almost all come with IDE, floppy, serial and parallel support. Often, boards are also available with SCSI, sound, network and video support built in. Don't buy one with on-board sound, because you don't need it on a server. If you get one with other on-board options, make sure the components are name-brand, integrated components. Also, make sure that all components can be disabled. Also, be absolutely certain that the video can be disabled via jumper! Failure of on-board video that cannot be disabled renders the entire motherboard useless. And, most of all, if you choose on-board components, make sure they save you money.

Brands

Intel, SuperMicro, Asus, Tyan, Acer, American Megatrends

Our choice

We selected the SuperMicro P6DBS. It features dual-Pentium II 450 support, built-in Adaptec Ultra-Wide SCSI and a RAIDport II upgrade slot.

Our cost

$380

Drive Controllers

IDE, EIDE, ATAPI, ULTRA ATA and ULTRA DMA: These are all enhanced variations of the Integrated Device Electronics (IDE) Standard. Don't use any of these devices (hard drives, CD-ROM drives or tape drives, *e.g.*) in a server for heavy use. Even drives with specifications that meet or exceed their SCSI equivalents won't perform even close to the SCSI devices. This is because IDE devices require much more from the CPU than SCSI devices do. This is by design of the standards, and it probably won't change anytime soon. SCSI devices will continue to outperform their IDE equivalents by a huge margin; they're usually twice as fast. Once you get past the learning curve for SCSI devices, they are easier to configure and are more standard than IDE. (SCSI CD-ROMs usually don't need special drivers, for example). Also, SCSI devices report their failures to the controller, making it possible to use a RAID controller. Buy SCSI for your server.

SCSI (Small Computer Systems Interface)—pronounced *scuzzy*, not *sexy* (although this was the intended pronunciation)—is the main alternative to IDE.

SCSI comes in many flavors. To make matters worse, new terms for types of SCSI have replaced the old terms. Below you will find all you need to know.

WARNING! A new type of SCSI can wreck your day if you are not careful. Until recently, "normal" SCSI devices were called *single-ended (SE)*, meaning that the voltage signal is compared to ground, and the resulting voltage is a signal. The new type is called *low-voltage differential (LVD)*. LVD's positive voltage signal is compared to the negative voltage signal, and the difference determines whether or not there is a signal. **LVD devices, controllers and terminators cannot coexist with SE devices; doing so may wreck all components.** If you are unsure what kind of component you have, don't install it. Go find out if it's SE or LVD.

How much do you need to know about SCSI? We'll give you the minimum you need to know for purchasing hardware and getting things started. Below are all of the SCSI Connectors:

- ❖ SCSI Types of SCSI:
- ❖ SCSI-1 5MB/Sec 8 bit SCSI bus
- ❖ SCSI-2 5MB/Sec 8 bit SCSI bus
- ❖ SCSI-2 Fast 10MB/Sec 8 bit SCSI bus
- ❖ SCSI-2 Fast Wide 20MB/Sec 16 bit SCSI bus
- ❖ SCSI Ultra 20MB/Sec 8 bit SCSI bus
- ❖ SCSI Ultra Wide 40MB/Sec 16 bit SCSI bus
- ❖ Ultra2 Narrow 40MB/Sec 8 bit SCSI bus
- ❖ Ultra2 Wide 80MB/sec 16 bit SCSI bus

Brands

Adaptec, BusLogic, Compaq, DPT, Digital Equipment (DEC), Mylex

Our choice

Our motherboard has built-in Adaptec SCSI. It features AIC-7895 dual channel, is SCSI dual-channel Ultra Wide and is essentially an Adaptec AHA-3940UW. However, our motherboard has a special slot, called a RAIDport II slot, that accepts a special Adaptec card, and suddenly our built-in SCSI becomes built-in RAID. This is both convenient and saves us money.

Our cost

After paying for our motherboard, this costs nothing extra.

RAID: Redundant Array of Independent Disks

Software RAID

Software RAID (stripe set) uses the operating system to create an array. This is not cool—it is a scam. This capability exists merely so that publishers of the operating system can claim RAID support. Software RAID cannot boot the operating system, so it provides no more protection than a stand-alone drive. Also, since the OS is not on the RAID, you don't gain any speed on most of the server. And, since the OS is busy handling the striping, it has less time to do real work. Absolutely do not use software RAID or stripe sets, no matter what anybody tells you.

Hardware RAID (Redundant Array of Independent Disks)

Hardware RAID systems are a better choice for nearly every application. Hardware RAID is based on two facts:

❖ Accessing multiple disks in parallel provides greater data throughput than a single disk can.

❖ Storing redundant data on multiple disks increases the security of that data.

With multiple disks and redundant data, your system can remain running properly, even while a failed disk is replaced.

Based upon your needs and budget, one of the seven types of hardware RAID will meet your security needs. These use different combinations of *striping*, *mirroring* and *parity* to improve performance and protect your data.

Striping is the process of writing data in sequential bands across several disks. For example, with three hard drives, striping would write data to a 500MB block on disk one, then continue writing data to the first 500MB block on disk two, then continue to fill the first 500MB of disk three, then return to disk one and write to the 500 – 1000MB block. It will continue this sequence until the write operation is complete. The size of this data block will vary, but will always be at least as large as a disk's sector size.

Mirroring essentially copies data from one disk onto another (similar to a mirror image, but without the reversals).

Parity is a means to insure that data is and remains accurate, similar to the parity used by some RAM chips.

RAID 0

RAID 0 uses only striping. This offers no redundancy, but all the disks can be read in parallel, decreasing access times. Although data isn't mirrored, a failed disk will only lose a part of the file, which (depending on the type of data) can probably be recreated from the surviving data on the other disks.

RAID 1

RAID 1 features mirroring, providing complete redundancy by writing the same data to multiple disks. Because these multiple writes are performed in parallel, you will notice no increase in write times. This is one of the surest ways to protect your data.

RAID 2

RAID 2 stripes data across multiple disks in block sizes of one bit, forcing every disk to be read by every read operation. In addition, RAID 2 requires an extra disk to store an error-correcting code. This code is created when data is written and checked when that data is read, insuring the data did not become corrupted. Because modern disk drives contain their own error-correcting code, RAID 2 is not a practical choice for most applications.

RAID 3

RAID 3 also stripes data across multiple disks, and it uses a parity disk, similar to RAID 2's error-correcting code. RAID 3 also reads every disk during a read operation.

RAID 4

RAID 4 is very similar to RAID 3, but the "stripe" width is larger than the disk sector size. This means that each block of data on a disk can be larger, which reduces the number of disks that need to spin for you to access specific data. However, because RAID 4 also uses a dedicated parity disk, this parity drive can quickly become a frustrating bottleneck.

RAID 5

RAID 5 stripes data across multiple drives using a stripe larger than the disk sector size, like RAID 4. It also uses parity, but unlike RAID 4's dedicated parity disk, RAID 5 stripes the parity across all disks. This provides the advantages of RAID 4 without the bottleneck created by the single parity disk.

RAID 5's biggest drawback is that write operations require two extra reads. To insure the integrity of the data, the system must read the old data block and the old parity block before writing the new parity block. However, you may not notice any performance penalty, since only about 10% of disk activity in a typical client/server system is write operations.

RAID 10

RAID 10 is a combination of RAID 0 (mirroring) and RAID 1 (striping). The disks are mirrored in pairs, then data is striped across them. This provides the benefits of each system: redundant data and maximum performance. For example, in a four-disk system, disks one and three will hold the same data, and disks two and four will also be mirrored. Data is then striped across disks one and two, with three and four being their mirrored pairs. This is one of the best applications of RAID, offering the performance advantages of other levels without the penalties.

Determining which RAID level is for you depends on your performance needs and your budget. For example, mirroring almost doubles the price of your system instantly, simply because you need twice as many hard drives. If your main goal is to install a RAID system while keeping costs low, then striping is your best option. At the other end of the spectrum, RAID 10's mirroring and striping offer unmatched security and performance, at a high price. What's best for you inherently depends on your system and how you will use that system.

RAID Controller Cards

RAID controllers are available from several manufacturers, for varying prices and with varying features.

Make sure the RAID controller you choose will suit your needs.

These are recommended features:

❖ It must have the ability to do RAID level five.

❖ Included software for easy array management on the server (in our case, Windows NT).

❖ Included or able to support a cache RAM module.

❖ Ability to support hot swapping of drives.

❖ All of the same concerns for SCSI cards, such as number of channels, drives supported, etc.

❖ Optionally, the RAID controller should support non-RAID and non-disk devices as well as the array. If the RAID controller cannot do so, you will have to purchase a separate SCSI controller for the other devices.

RAID Upgrade Cards

RAID upgrade cards are available for a number of server motherboards. These cards offer the chance to use a motherboard's built-in SCSI as the RAID controller.

"Zero channel" RAID solution: At least one of Intel's server boards supports this option. These upgrade cards are available from AMI (American Megatrends) and Mylex. These cards go into a PCI slot.

RAIDport (RAID port II, RAIDport III): RAIDport cards are RAID upgrade cards (from Adaptec) that cost much less than regular RAID controllers. This card requires a special connector on the motherboard and the motherboard must have Adaptec SCSI on board.

RAID sub-system solutions

Some manufacturers offer a RAID sub-system controller. This device usually fits into a 5.25-inch bay and has a front control panel on it. This is the RAID controller, and it connects via PCI, SCSI or maybe a serial port for remote control when used externally. Enlight is an example of a company that produces these devices.

Brands

Adaptec, Mylex, DEC, IBM, Compaq, Micropolis, Symbios Logic, BusLogic, Unisys, Clarion, DPT, and American Megatrends (AMI)

Our choice

The Adaptec ARO-1130 SA for RAIDport II

Our cost

$299

Hard Drives

Sustained Data Transfer Rate

This is the rate (usually listed in megabytes per second) at which the drive is capable of delivering a continuous flow of data to the controller. You must have a controller that is capable of accepting the data at this rate or your drive won't function properly. 40 MB/sec. is an acceptable rate of sustained data transfer capabilities. Keep in mind, like fuel economy and tire tread, real-world performance may vary.

Burst/Maximum Transfer Rate

This is the rate at which data is bursted to the controller's bus. This can never be maintained; it's like sprinting the 100-yard dash versus a marathon. Don't use this to measure a drive's performance until the other three criteria are compared. Your drive controller should be able to accept data at or near the burst data transfer rate of your drive, though it's alright if the controller is a little slower.

Seek Time

This is how long the hard drive takes to find the start of the chunk of data you are writing or reading. The biggest bottleneck is not moving the head to the correct cylinder, but waiting for the correct location on the platters to come around for the drive heads. This is called *rotational latency*. Server drives should have seek times of less than 10 millisecond (ms).

Spindle Speed

The spindle speed is the rate at which the platters inside the drive mechanism spin, measured in RPMs. Currently, 3.5" drives typically come in 5,400, 7,200, and 10,000 RPM varieties. Why faster? The drive head doesn't have to wait as long for a sector to come around! However, faster drives are expensive and tend to be physically thicker, noisier, and they generate more heat. 7,200 RPM drives currently offer the most bang for the buck.

Diameter

Hard Drives are available in 5 1/4", 3 1/2", 2 1/2" diameter sizes. 3.5 is the most common size and is the optimum price/performance mark. Don't buy a 5.25-inch hard drive! These drives may seem like a cheap alternative, but they don't perform well. You just can't get the spindle speed and head tracking performance with such large platters, so don't waste your money.

Cache

Get at least 512K or larger cache on each drive. This is critical to high performance, so don't skimp here.

Brands

Consider Quantum, Fujitsu, Seagate, Western Digital, and IBM hard drives

Our choice

We will install three Quantum 4500UW, 4.5 GB each, featuring 7,200 RPM, 7.5ms seek time, 512 K cache and Ultra-Wide Single-Ended SCSI.

Our cost

$239 each = $717

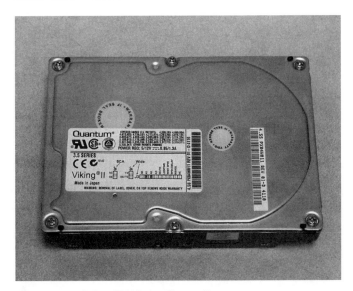

Removable Drive Brackets

Removable drive brackets are necessary if you'll remove a hard drive while a server is running. It's risky to disconnect and reconnect the standard power and SCSI cables, and it's also risky to root around with a screwdriver inside the case of a server that's running. To solve all of these issues, buy hard drive brackets. Many removable-drive brackets have a key lock and a standard interface. This works pretty easily: Buy one more drive and one more cartridge than you need. Install the receiving end of each cartridge into a bay in the server case. Install each drive into a cartridge. Then, install each cartridge into a slot.

Brands

Data-Port® Brand: Data-Port brand removable drive brackets (also called drive racks, drive frames or drive trays) from CRU Technologies have set the standard for do-it-yourself removable hard drives. Data-Port compatible drive brackets are even available from other companies!

Smart Shuttle® Brand: Smart Shuttle also provides a removable drive solution. These brackets are a little more pricey than the Data-Ports.

Eagle Nest Products from Exabyte: These have been discontinued. This is very unfortunate, because Exabyte is a large company and a respected name in the industry. Eagle Nest products were very expensive. If you are offered a dozen or so Eagle Nest Brackets that are cheap and are still new in the package, consider using them in your server. Otherwise, choose one of the others.

These and other generic-type drive brackets are available, but these brands are better sellers.

If you choose a generic brand, be sure they are high quality and are readily available, in case you want to expand.

Our choice

We have chosen three of the Data-Port V series removable drive brackets for our server.

Our cost

$140 each = $420

(Optional: One extra cartridge insert: $80)

Removable Media

Floppy drives

Get a 3.5-inch floppy drive and don't pay more than $25.

Brands

Sony, Panasonic, Teac, Mitsumi, Epson, Goldstar, NEC

Our choice

Mitsumi

Cost

$20

CD-ROM Drives

Get a bootable SCSI CD-ROM drive. This drive is not for sharing out to other computers across the network; it's just for local use. Buy a 16x or faster drive that's bootable. Don't bother with a much faster drive, unless it's only a few dollars more. Consider buying a CD-RW read capable CD-ROM drive. This will allow you to read re-writable CD media and may be useful in the future.

CD-ROM Towers

This is where you put the CDs that you are sharing across the network. This is a special kind of server. Don't try to make your file server your CD-ROM server as well. Keep in mind that this is different than a CD-ROM "jukebox;" in a jukebox drive only one disc is accessible at a time. In a tower, all are accessible at the same time.

Brands

Sony, Toshiba, Panasonic, Teac, Plextor, Pioneer, NEC

Our choice

We have chosen a SCSI (narrow, single ended) Toshiba XM-6201 32x CD-ROM drive. It reads CD-RW and is bootable.

Cost

$110

Tape Drives

You need a tape drive. Yes, a RAID will save you from hard-drive failure, a UPS will save you from a power failure, and your anti-virus software can protect you from viruses. But how do you protect yourself from the worst destroyer of data: human error? You will need to back up all or most of your files on a daily (or more often) basis. Not only that, but you need to store the backups on a permanent or long-term basis.

Let's take a look at the tape drive scenario. The boss will ask for stuff like this: "Hey, I wrote a letter to the CEO of Zeppelin Corporation and I accidentally deleted it. Anyway, you guys have backups, don't you? I need that letter restored. The Hindenburg deal is pending on it. If I don't get that letter back, everything could go down in flames! Send me an e-mail when you get that. Thanks." Sounds easy: just get yesterday's tape and be done with it. Little do you know he accidentally deleted it a year and a half ago! Anyway, you get the idea. Keep your tapes until..., well, forever. Also, if your company frequently creates electronic finished products, documents or completed files, consider archiving them on CD-Recordable. Keep all this in a fireproof vault.

What if you are really concerned about your data? Keep copies at an offsite storage facility. Several places will store your valuable media. Michigan Natural Storage, (616) 241-1619, will store items in unused mine shafts in Grand Rapids, Michigan. This might actually survive a nuclear blast!

Now that you know why you need tape-backup, let's pick one out. Unfortunately, I can think of at least a dozen types of tape, and none of them has totally beat out the others. These five are the most prevalent.

Types of Tape Drives

Travan

These are the "TR"-type tapes, one of the cheapest types of tape drives available, although the tapes cost more than the others. Travan is also a very mature product, indicating reliability. It is unlikely that any Travan-type drive will ever hold much more than 8 or 10 GB of compressed data. These come in varying capacities and offer the most "bang for the buck." These cost about $300 for a TR-4, holding 8 GB compressed and transfering 60 MB per minute. Tapes cost about $32 each, equating to about $4/GB.

8mm

The tapes are just high-grade 8mm camcorder tapes. I recently procured some 3M 8mm data tapes and called 3M just to make sure. They are extremely high grade and produce an excellent picture and sound in Hi8 video systems, as well. (Consider asking the manufacturer before using data tapes in video equipment!) However, don't try to use videotape in your 8mm data drive! Your data will not be secure unless you use the correct type of tape! 8mm tape drives are available for $900 for a 14-GB compressed capacity drive and move 60 MB per minute. Tapes cost about $20 each, equaling about $1.42/GB.

4mm/DAT (DDS)

The same is true for Digital Audio Tape data drives. These are just high-grade, data-certified media, and would work great in a DAT audio drive, although the DAT is rarely used as a consumer product. Don't use the audio versions of these tapes in your data drive! Your data will not be secure! DDS drives hold up to 24 GB of compressed data, transfer up to 144 MB/min and cost about $800. Tape changers are available: a six- or eight-tape changer costs about $2,500! Tapes cost about $20 each, for about $0.83/GB.

DLT

Digital Linear Tape (DLT) is high capacity, very fast and very expensive. These are highly reliable with a very high capacity, around 70 GB per tape (compressed), and they transfer 600 MB/min, but cost over $5,000! The next generation may yield even higher capacity. Tapes cost about $95, equating to $1.35/GB.

AIT

This new type of 8mm high-speed/high-capacity drive is cool because it's available with Memory-In-Cassette (MIC). The memory contains a directory of the files on the tape, so your drive can find files in a hurry. They move 360 MB/min. The drive costs about $3,000. A tape costs about $80 for 50 MB compressed capacity, equaling about $1.60 /GB.

Autoloaders (Tape Changers, Tape Libraries)

How big a drive do you need? Buying 100% of your hard drive capacity will give you one unattended backup; this is the minimum capacity. If you are going to use the tape drive to back up multiple servers or workstations across the network, buy a bigger drive. Plain and simple, the larger the tape, the less often a person has to change the tapes. However, you can compromise. You can buy a tape drive autoloader! Autoloaders are great for unattended backups, and hold from two to 200 tapes, depending on the size (and the price). Just about all kinds of tape drives are available in an autoloader except the Travan. Travan tapes aren't designed to be automatically ejected; the user pushes them in and pulls them out by hand.

Which one should you buy so that you're not stuck with an obsolete drive? Don't worry about using your tape in somebody else's drive—these are *your* backups. Pick one that's cost effective: for extremely high end, buy a DLT; for low end, get a Travan style. DDS seems to offer the most performance for the price.

Brands

Sony, Seagate, Exabyte, Hewlett Packard, Quantum, Compaq are all good brands of tape drives.

Our choice

This was tough. Since we couldn't decide, we will be featuring both a Travan TR-4 and an HP DDS drive.

Our cost

$300 for Travan; $800 for the DDS drive

Our DDS drive

Our Travan 4 drive

Special Software: Seagate Software's BackUp Exec (www.seagatesoftware.com) is one of the best software applications for tape back up. Computer Associate's Cheyenne ArcServe (www.cai.com) product is also one of the best.

RAM

In the early days, computing was unreliable. ENIAC, the first fully electronic computer, was very unreliable—vacuum tubes burned out every few minutes. Fortunately, today's computers are much more reliable, which creates a strange irony. The ENIAC could be counted on to be unreliable. When it broke, it was really broken; that is, it needed parts replaced before it would function at all. Eckert and Mauchly don't know how lucky they were. Today's computers are so reliable that they almost never pour smoke out the back and need new parts. However, when things go wrong, they only go wrong *a little bit!* The irony is that this is worse! The high reliability is not high enough to produce absolute perfection. As computers get faster and performance demands increase, so does the amount of shear data that needs to be processed. For example, in a 100-MB .TIF image file, not one of the almost one billion bits can be wrong—NOT ONE—or the entire file could be corrupt. Engineers have devised ingenious ways to combat incorrect bits. (Amazingly enough, we borrow this technology from nature: DNA tricodes are the most ingeniously effective yet simple correction algorithm for stored data ever created). The first area of incorrect bits to be addressed is on the network wire or the telephone wire. The longer distance the data travels, the more likely that you will lose some data bits. Network protocols have error detection and correction built in. Modems use error checking and correcting protocols. Now, so does RAM!

You must have Error Checking and Correcting (ECC) Memory for maximum uptime.

However, your motherboard, your Pentium II chip, and your memory must all be ECC compatible (this is a special type of memory). Also, you must enable this option in the BIOS setup.

RAM (Random Access Memory) has had a problem for a while. No solution has been presented to resolve the following issues:

When a user picks up a memory module, none of following information is printed on it: capacity (in Megabytes), parity/ECC able, speed (in nanoseconds), type (EDO or other) or the manufacturer.

Worst of all, a computer can't automatically determine that information, either. Nor can the BIOS set the timing and other settings automatically. But now we have a solution: the Serial Presence Detect (SPD) module. This is a new module that is built into the DIMM. The BIOS can not only retrieve critical information about the DIMM, but can now automatically optimize a system for speed and reliability. Oh, and now your computer can tell you who made the DIMMs that are installed your computer. This is not as useful as automatic performance optimization, but it's there anyway (and is pretty cool). Buy SPD DIMMs for ease of use and painless optimum performance. See http://www.corsairmicro.com/SPD.htm for more information.

SIMMs (Single Inline Memory Modules)

These are memory chips on a miniature card.

One SIMM fills one slot, and each slot represents a bank (on 486 and Pentium motherboards). SIMMs usually must be installed in identically matched pairs.

DIMMs vs. SIMMs

DIMMs are just like SIMMs, but one DIMM (Dual Inline Memory Module) fills a slot. One slot fills two banks on motherboards with DIMM slots. This is why you only need to insert DIMMs one at a time.

Standard RAM (Fast Page)

This is the "normal" type of RAM. It's also referred to as non-parity.

Parity (Fast Page)

This type of SIMM has an extra chip on board to serve as a check bit for the other eight. Plain "parity" memory is Fast Page and can go in a "non-parity" board. Parity memory and the associated motherboards disappeared for a while. When a parity error would occur, the BIOS would throw up a warning screen that said "parity error." This was not all that useful; if you continued and saved your file, it might be corrupted. If you rebooted on the spot, this didn't really help you any. The parity option was unavailable for a while, and RAM manufacturers got better. Non-parity memory worked well and didn't have many errors at the slow processor speeds.

ECC (error checking and correcting)

Another type of error correcting RAM is now quite popular in PCs. As RAM speeds increased, engineers and users feared system failures that could cause loss of data in critical applications. To combat this, they implemented ECC in PCs, which corrects some RAM errors and allows the computer to continue in operation while reporting the failure to the user. ECC is awesome and costs almost nothing extra. However, you must have chipset support (like the Intel 440BX), processor LII ECC cache support (Pentium II 300 and faster), and the options must be enabled in the BIOS setup.

EDO (Extended Data Out)

This type of RAM is faster than Fast Page and has become quite popular. Parity EDO SIMMs are also available, but are extremely rare. EDO DIMMs are commonplace and are available with ECC.

SDRAM (Synchronous Dynamic RAM)

This stuff is fast. This is now the *de facto* standard. SDRAM is so fast that no other types of RAM are common.

PC100

This compliance level assures that the RAM will work in a 100-MHz bus. (Warning: 100-MHz SDRAM is different than PC100-compliant SDRAM. The chips on a 100-MHz DIMM run at 100 MHz, but the interface is only capable of 66 MHz. Get PC100 compliant RAM!) PC100 RAM can be run in any speed computer bus.

Interleaving is a process by which the CPU accesses RAM so that the opposite bank is accessed while the current bank refreshes. This can improve performance by as much as 10%, but can require DIMMs to be installed in pairs. This also requires support from the motherboard's chipset and must be enabled in the BIOS setup.

Buy memory that is approved for use with your motherboard. Some motherboard manufacturers, like Tyan, approve particular makes and models of memory modules for use in their motherboards. Follow their recommendations for maximum performance. However, "bulk" RAM is available everywhere. Normally, generic products are not recommended. Since RAM is such a well-defined component of a PC, bulk RAM has a stronghold on the market. If you choose bulk memory, buy it from a reliable vendor. Bulk RAM from a reliable vendor will perform exactly like name brand RAM.

Brands

Corsair, Kingston, Micron (also called Crucial)

Our choice

Bulk RAM—Two 64-MB SDRAM DIMMS, featuring ECC and PC100 compliant

Our cost

$85 each = $170

The Processor

How do you select a processor? There are three good choices for servers: Pentium Pro, Pentium II and Pentium II Xeon. Which one is the best choice? Let's take a look:

Pentium Pro

This is the first processor with a level-II cache "on-die"—meaning it runs at the same speed as the processor. In the Pentium Pro's case, this was up to 200 MHz. It is also optimized for 32-bit code (i.e., native Windows NT and Novell 4.11) operation, but chokes to a halt when running 16-bit code (i.e., Windows 95, or older Windows and DOS programs). The Pro uses socket technology (it lays flat against the board) and is designed for servers and for multiprocessing on a large scale. An Intel server is available that contains a few hundred Pentium Pro chips. This chip is very expensive to build and the price reflects that. If you have two or more of these and want to build a server, they are an excellent choice. However, if you are building (and buying) from scratch, you'll get more bang for your buck from Pentium II chips.

Pentium II

This chip is the first in the *slot* series and has been accused of looking like an Atari cartridge. This chip is faster than the Pentium Pro in clock speed (up to 333 MHz), but its L-II cache is off-die and only half the clock speed. This chip does have the advantage of a cheaper design (and selling price), as well as optimization for both 16-bit and 32-bit code (it runs Windows 95 just as well as it runs Windows NT). The Pentium II has been criticized as a step backward in technology.

Pentium II, second generation

This is the 350-, 400- and 450-MHz varieties. These chips are special because they use a 100-MHz bus speed. Still, the L-II cache only runs at half clock speed. On the fastest PII, that's only 225 MHz, about the same as the Pentium Pro!

Pentium II Xeon

This is a brand new chip from Intel which promises to be nothing short of amazing. Like the Pentium II, it uses slot technology, 16-bit and 32-bit code optimization, and along with some very useful intelligent manageability features, the goose's golden egg: full-speed cache! Yes, 400-MHz Level-II cache! This chip is relatively cheap to produce, works great in multiprocessor systems, and is just plain awesome. However, they are pricey compared to regular PII CPUs.

How many Processors? Which kind of processors? These are almost the same question, a question of money, and how to get the most for your money. Two fast Pentium IIs are likely to perform as well as one Xeon, and two slow P IIs are likely to be as fast as one fast PII. For our design, we have chosen a PII 400 ECC configuration with a board that will support two 400-MHz chips if we upgrade. If you go dual processor from the start, purchase the board with the chips to guarantee compatibility, and you may also get a discount on the total package. If you are upgrading to dual processor, make sure they are compatible with each other. (See http://support.intel.com/support/processors/pentiumII/ for a note on mixing processors on a motherboard.)

Choose CPUs according to your needs. This is the hardest factor to judge. Buy CPUs that offer the most for your money. The price difference from two 233s to two 266s might be only $20, but to get two 300s may cost $260 more. Also remember that hard drive speed is far more important than your processor speed. If you are unsure what processor configuration to buy, get a single 266 ECC system with a 440 BX chipset. Spend the extra money on bigger and faster hard drives and a bigger, faster tape drive.

Brands

Intel

Our choice

Pentium II 400 MHz, Boxed* CPU

*Boxed CPUs from Intel come with the fan and heat sink already attached. They also come with a three-year warranty. OEM CPUs come bare, with a one-year warranty. Frequently, the price of a boxed Intel chip is about the same as an OEM chip plus a fan. Be sure to get a high-quality ball bearing fan and heat sink if you select an OEM CPU.

Our cost

$469

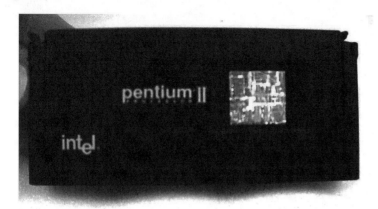

Heat, your enemy, and how to get rid of it

Fans, Fans, Fans

Put a heat sink directly on the CPU. Be sure to use heat transfer grease or make sure the heat sink has a heat transfer pad. Attach a quality, ball-bearing fan to the heat sink. CPU fans and heat sinks are usually available as a unit. Boxed Intel CPUs come with a fan and heat sink specially designed for the CPU. The price of a boxed CPU is about the same as a CPU and fan/heat sink purchased separately! Always buy a boxed CPU if you can. If you cannot, AAVID makes the best CPU fan/heat sink assemblies.

You should also get a fan for each hard drive in the computer. If you get internal drive bracket pullouts, make sure they include a fan. Quality drive bracket pullout fans are temperature controlled and run only when the drives get hot—pretty cool!

Make sure you have a quality power supply with a fan. Some power supplies can inform the computer if their fans fail and they begin to overheat.

The case must also have a large exhaust fan with a dust filter. Somehow, all that heat needs to be removed from the case. Rear fans, front fans, fans that fit into 5.25" bays, or even ones that fit into rear expansion slots can help you dissipate heat.

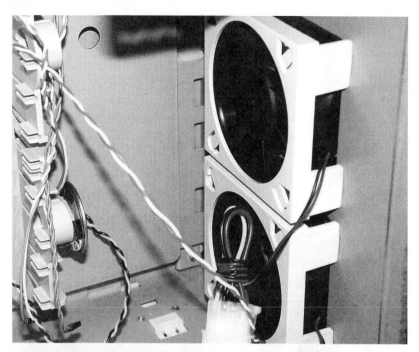

Finally, you also have to cool the room. Air conditioning is a must for server rooms. Humidity is also a concern; don't set equipment on a bare cement floor (get a cabinet with a rack!). Server rooms seem to generate their own heat.

Modem

Dial in using RAS (Remote Access Service): Wouldn't it be nice to be able to manage the network from anywhere? That's what RAS is for. All you need is another computer (with NT remote management software on it), modems in both computers and a phone line in between. After enabling RAS under Windows NT, you can do quite a bit from home (or wherever you happen to be). Also, users can be granted access to the network using RAS and can work just like they are at the office, just a little slower. Modems and phone lines are dirt cheap. Get at least one RAS connection. (Alert! Put a highly secret password on the RAS Administrator connection service. A user can do a lot of damage with a RAS connection with Administrative privileges, like format a hard drive, introduce a virus or grant themselves future Administrative privileges. Be careful!) Buy a US Robotics (USR) brand modem from 3Com. Don't buy a "WinModem!" It is not a normal modem, and it doesn't have a controller. The USR Sportster 33.6/56K is a highly supported modem and has proven itself to be very popular. Choose a US Robotics, Hayes, or other quality modem for your dial-in access.

Brands

US Robotics (3Com), Hayes, Diamond, Motorola, Boca, and Compaq

Our choice

We have chosen to access our network using PPTP across our ISDN connection.

Network Interface Card (NIC)

Ethernet/Fast Ethernet

You need a network card (or two for redundancy): Intel and 3Com make more network cards than anybody. Both 3Com and Intel offer special network cards for servers that offer load balancing and fault tolerance. However, rumor has it that 3Com's driver is in its infancy, and Intel's technology is also new. Since the redundancy and load balancing technologies are new, and NIC's are highly reliable components, we have chosen to have a single NIC in our server. Choose PCI over ISA for better performance.

Brands

Intel EtherExpress Pro 100+, 3Com Fast Etherlink XL PCI, Cabletron, Compaq, Digital Equipment (DEC), Hewlett-Packard (HP), IBM, Linksys, Kingston, Standard Microsystems (SMC), Adaptec

Our choice

Intel EtherExpress Pro 100+

Our cost

$85

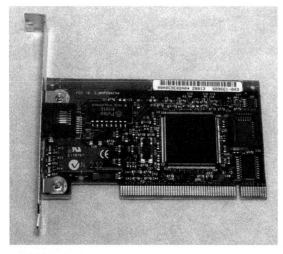

ISDN Adapter

This comes in two forms: an ISDN Modem, which is just a modem for an ISDN phone line. The other kind is an ISDN terminal adapter, which keeps an open connection across the ISDN circuit just like it's a network connection. 3Com and other companies have invented stand-alone boxes that are just like terminal adapters and dial-on-demand. When do you need which one? The modem provides Internet connectivity for computers on the inside, but doesn't make a permanent connection for a company to put up a Website. That's what the terminal adapter is for! It provides the permanent connection. ISDN is useful to connect two remote office sites together, and ISDN also can provide a fast ISP connection.

Special Note On Who's Not Your Enemy

Static electricity:
Rarely does static cause problems, but when handling components, always wear a wrist strap that grounds your body. If you do this, you need not concern yourself with static.

Electromagnetic Fields:
There's a common misconception about EMFs. They are a concern in networking, but they don't damage things. Eqiupment just doesn't work properly while being affected by EMFs. Moving the component away from the source of the EMF will always correct the problem. Avoid placing a server near a large power transformer that supplies a building or other heavy-duty equipment.

EMF concerns for networks:
Always keep cabling away from any EMF source. Avoid power circuits of any kind. For more information, look up EIA/TIA standards for installing category five cabling in a building. The rule of thumb is not to run any cable longer than 328 feet (100 meters). Don't coil the cable. Don't run the cable within 12 inches of fluorescent lights or their ballasts. Don't get anywhere near a building's power transformer! How can you tell if the cable path is causing your problem? Either move the cable or try a different cable path with the same equipment. If you are really fussy, testers can be purchased, but these cost thousands of dollars and require professional training. Cable installation is a specialty in itself, so call the experts for big jobs. Local companies frequently install cabling equipment made by companies like Belden, Berk-Tek, Otronics, Hubbell, Leviton and Panduit. Some national and regional companies, like Lucent Technologies and TDS Telecom, are getting into the cabling business.

Special Note

In the past, the FCC has required that computers built from parts must pass FCC interference testing and certification. This took six months, by which time the server was frequently obsolete! Recently, the law has changed to reflect the rapid pace of the computer industry. Quite simply, as long as the components themselves have passed FCC testing, the computer will meet FCC regulations. Look for certification labels on all your components or packaging. Otherwise, contact the manufacturer of the component to verify that it has passed certification.

User Input

Keyboard

Your keyboard will use one of three types of connectors: AT, PS/2 or USB. The first two are the same electronically and are easily converted with an adapter. Some keyboards can also adapt from AT or PS/2 to USB, which is becoming tomorrow's standard.

Brands

Mitsumi, Keytronics, Acer, Microsoft, Qtronix

Our choice

Mitsumi AT-compatible, with PS/2 connector

Our cost

$20

Mouse

We also need a mouse. Those new scrolling-wheel mice are pretty cool. Otherwise, any type of mouse will do. Mice are available with PS/2, serial and USB connections.

Brands

Mitsumi, Logitech, Microsoft, Kensington

Our choice

Microsoft Intellimouse

Our cost

$35

User Output

Video Card (Display adapter)

We need a video card. We aren't too concerned about fast video—we just don't want it to slow down the system. The video card should be AGP or PCI, not ISA.

We need a medium amount of Video RAM so we can get decent resolution. We need at least two megabytes of Video RAM, but we don't have to have dual-ported Video RAM. EDO, SDRAM or SGRAM is acceptable.

We need a high refresh rate. Be sure your video card can do 70Hz or higher at a resolution of 1024 x 768.

Brands

ATI, Diamond, Matrox, STB, NumberNine (#9), Hercules

Our choice

Matrox Mystique G220, 2 MB VRAM

Our cost

$65

Monitor

We need a monitor. One that can support a refresh rate of 70Hz or higher at 1024 x 768 will be all we need.

Brands

Sony, Samsung, CTX, Mag Innovision, Mitsubishi, NEC, Viewsonic, Optiquest, Princeton, Philips, Panasonic, KDS

Our choice

Mitsubishi 15" 1280x1024

Our cost

$149

KVM (Keyboard/Video/Mouse) Switch Boxes

If you want to hook multiple servers and PCs to one monitor, mouse, and keyboard, only one brand has proven itself as superior: Raritan. Raritan uses one emulation chip per port; other boxes use time slicing through one chip. Without a dedicated chip for each port, there's a risk of causing a computer to crash unexpectedly. If you want a KVM switch box, get a Raritan or other brand using a dedicated emulation chip on every port.

Now we have all are parts! Let's move on to Chapter 4 for assembly.

Chapter 4:
Assembling the Server

F

irst, let's open our packages and see what we have:

The Case

The case has seven exposed 5.25" bays and a 3.5" floppy bay behind a locking door.

Case from the front, feet in, door closed, sides on

Case from front, door open, all blanks in place

On the back, we have a big hole, a smaller hole, two fans, and several expansion slots with blank covers in place.

The back of our empty case

Let's open the case. Remove the screws on the back that hold the side panels.

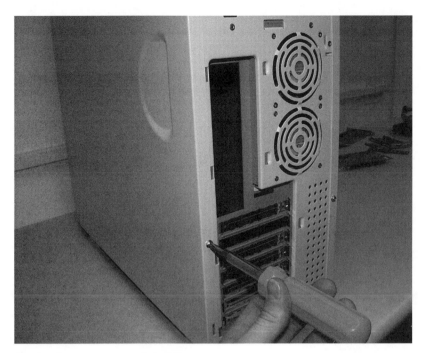

Back of case, unscrewing sides

Next, let's pull off the sides and look inside:

Removing the side of the case

Inside we find an assortment of parts. Our case has:

- ❖ One 3.5" bay

- ❖ Seven 5.25" bays

- ❖ A removable bracket for two internal 3.5" hard drives

- ❖ Holes for motherboard standoffs to be installed into

- ❖ Wires for attaching lights, switches and the speaker

❖ Four fans installed in the case

❖ A bag of parts

We don't, however, have a power supply.

A side view of our open case

Go ahead and remove the front panel. It pops off from the bottom.

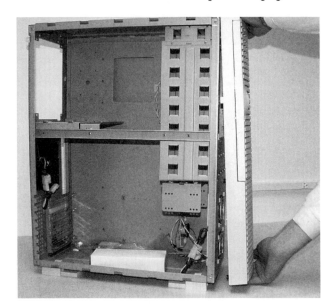

Front of case being pulled off, side view

Also, remove the 3.5" drive bracket by pushing in the tab and pulling the bracket out. Throw this piece in your spare computer parts bin. We won't be using it for our server.

Drive cage, tab indicated

Next, let's examine the parts inside:

The stuff in the case

We have:

* ❖ Keys to the case.

❖ The case manual.

❖ A floppy drive cable.

❖ An ATX backplate (this will go into the smaller hole in the back of the case).

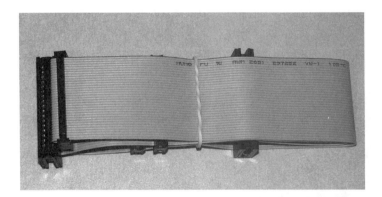

❖ About 16 of these rails.

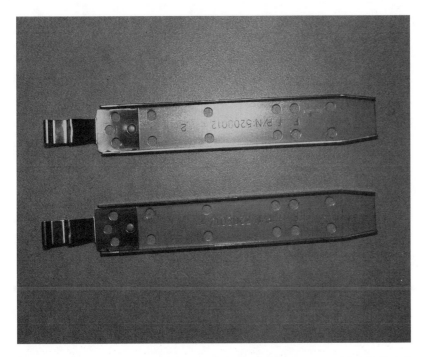

We also have a small bag of parts containing many of the following.

❖ Two types of standoffs: the kind that accepts a screw and the kind that has a clip.

Screw-in motherboard standoff

Slide-in motherboard standoff

❖ Self-adhesive tie-downs, and tie straps to go with them.

Tie down

Tie strap

❖ Fine threaded screws.

- Coarse threaded screws, some with a smooth head (underneath) and some with a locking pattern under the head.

Coarse thread screw, flat under head (left)
Coarse thread screw, locks under head (right)

Next, look at the inside of the case. Near the top of the case are a power switch, a reset switch, a hard drive light and a power light.

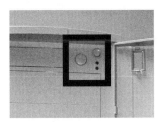

Power switch, etc

Wires run from the top to the bottom. Find the other ends of the wires, and examine the connectors. All of them should have labels, like this.

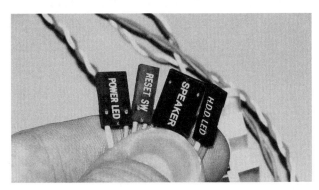

The case switch and LED connectors

Notice that one connector goes to the speaker, which is in the front of the case near the front fans.

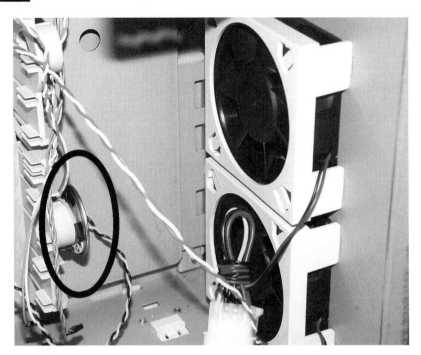

Front Speaker

We will attach these connectors to the motherboard later. Prepare the case by removing the appropriate number of drive bay covers from the front of the case.

On the inside, remove the metal braces from the case. They are part of the manufacturing process; they aren't necessary. Wiggle them back and forth until they fall out.

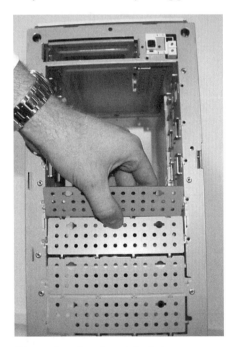

Removing front metal plates

The plastic ones just pop right out:

Removing front plastic plates

Now that we've removed just about everything from the case, let's start putting things inside it!

The Power Supply

Open up the power supply box:

Power supply, still in box

Look at the power supply. Notice that it is extremely heavy and looks like two power supplies in one.

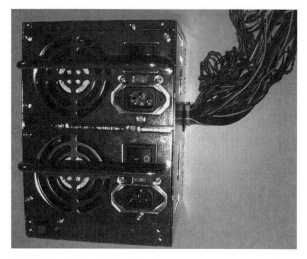

Power supply on bench

We also have an installation guide for the power supply.

Notice all of the different connectors.

A standard ATX power connector goes to the motherboard:

You'll also see about 10 standard power connectors and a miniature power connector for the floppy drive:

Accessory power and mini accessory power connectors

We also have some strange-looking connectors. One of them will require special treatment for our ATX case.

You've probably never seen an owner's manual for a power supply before. It's not just a good idea to read this, it's required to get the power supply to work. Inside, we find information about the extra wiring. We need to make a minor modification for our power supply to work. This power supply is designed for industrial applications as well as for servers. Our modification is stated explicitly in the owner's manual.

We need to splice these two wires together. (If your case is ATX, but has an AT power switch in addition to the ATX power switch, attach these leads to that switch and turn it on. Don't cut and splice them if you have the additional switch.)

Black and White wires, plain

We need a standard screw-on splice connector, often used for house wiring. These can be found at any hardware store.

Wire connector, for splicing

Using side cutters, cut off the ends of the wires. Using a standard wire stripper (or if you're careful, using side cutters), strip about ½ inch off the ends of both wires.

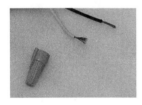

Black and White wires, after stripping

Next, twist the wires together in the clockwise direction. This will make it easy to screw on the splice connector.

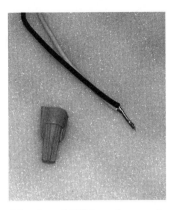

Black and White wires, twisted together

Now, screw on the insulator cap (splice connector):

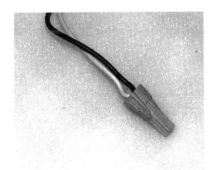

Black and White wires with splice connector installed

Our power supply is ready to be installed. Tip it up into the side of the case.

Power supply, being tipped into place

Pull it to the back of the case:

Power supply being pulled into place

Using four of the locking screws, screw the power supply into place, as marked in the photo:

Power supply being screwed in

Power supply screw mounts

Go ahead and see how each power supply swaps out. (In a failure, be sure that the failed power supply is turned off and that the other one remains on.)

Unscrew the power supply cartridge from the housing.

Unscrewing a power supply module

Next, pull out the power supply module:

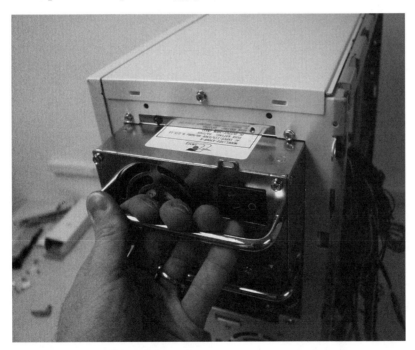

Pulling out a power supply

Notice that the back of the power supply has a cartridge insert connector:

A removed power supply module

Okay, now put it back in and screw it down.

The Motherboard

Let's open our motherboard box and see what's inside.

Supermicro Motherboard boxtop

Inside, we have the motherboard, of course:

We also have two books and a CD-ROM,

and some parts:

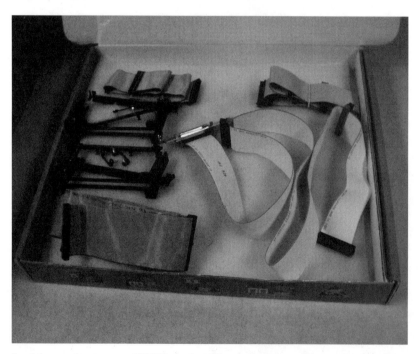

Inside, we have two CPU bracket kits, a floppy cable, an IDE cable, a 50-pin SCSI cable (narrow) and a 68-pin SCSI cable (wide). Don't get confused: the "narrow" SCSI cable is actually physically wider than the "wide" SCSI cable!

Our CPU bracket kits look like this:

CPU mounting kit

We'll install the CPU mounting brackets later. First, let's take a tour around the motherboard.

It has three ISA slots:

and four 32-bit PCI slots,

one of which is the RAIDport II expansion slot. It is an extended 32-bit PCI slot, and it looks a lot like the new 64-bit PCI slots:

Next to the PCI slots is the AGP port:

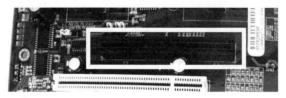

AGP port, closeup

On the back, we have the standard connectors that will fit into the ATX opening in the back of the case:

ATX connections on motherboard

From left to right: PS/2 keyboard and mouse connectors, USB connectors, one parallel port and two serial ports.

On the board, find the DIMM slots for the RAM:

DIMM slots (marked)

Also locate the IDE connectors (although we won't be using them) and the floppy connector:

These are the SCSI connectors:

SCSI connectors on the motherboard

NOTE: You can't use both the 50-pin narrow (the larger connector) and the 68-pin wide (the smaller connector) directly next to it at the same time. You must choose one of the two connectors. You can still use the outer 68-pin wide connector at the same time as either of the other two. The channels are separated with markings in the picture. Do not connect to more than one connector in each box that is drawn in the photo.

Near the bottom, we have the pin connectors for the LEDs, switches, and the speaker.

LED pin connectors on the motherboard

We also have the CPU slots and the power supply connector:

CPU slots and Power supply connector

Installing the CPU

We need to set the clock of the CPU. In the center of our motherboard (and in the manual) is the table of jumpers, which indicates the jumper patterns that activate the different CPU speeds:

Motherboard speed jumpers

This corresponds to the speed jumpers, located between the AGP port and CPU number one:

For our 400-MHz CPU, we have set jumpers JB1, JB2, and JB4 to achieve "4x," which is 4 x 100. The 100-MHz bus speed will be set automatically by the presence of a 100-MHz bus-capable CPU.

Special Note

What happens if you set the CPU clock too high (say, at 6x)? First, you will void the warranty of the CPU. Second, the CPU might get very hot and could be damaged. Also, the computer may be unstable, and you might reduce the lifespan of the CPU. It is highly recommended that you use the correct CPU clock speed for the chip that's installed.

Attaching the CPU bracket:

Place both of the stud mounts through the holes on the bottom of the motherboard for CPU slot number one.

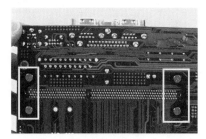

CPU mounts, both CPU studs installed, bottom view

Turn the motherboard back over, holding the stud mounts in place as you lower the board.

Top view of motherboard with studs installed

Place the bracket on top of the stud mounts. One side of the CPU slot will be free of components and will have space for the fan and bracket:

CPU fan area indicated

Be sure the notch on the CPU bracket faces towards the fan side!

Now, tighten down the bracket, starting all the screws before finishing any. Don't make these screws very tight, just hand tight.

CPU mount being attached to Motherboard

The RAM DIMMs

Now is a good time to install the memory. Look at the DIMMs. Note the two notches in the bottom of each one: one in the center and one off to the side. This prevents them from going in the wrong way.

Before installation, flip the DIMM slot tabs out on the motherboard. Select one of the DIMMs and simply push it straight down into the DIMM slot until the tabs snap around the DIMM. Be certain to install the first DIMM in the first slot on the motherboard. This slot is usually slot "0".

First DIMM being installed

Do the same thing with the second DIMM.

Second DIMM being installed

The CPU

Open the CPU box.

Inside we find a CPU, an instruction manual with warranty guide, a CPU fan power connector, two fan clips, two fan clip pegs, and the "Intel inside" sticker.

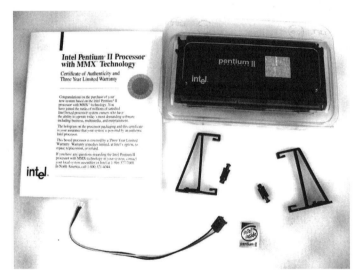

Take the two CPU fan clip pegs and insert them into the holes in the motherboard.

CPU mount pegs

CPU fan peg about to go in

CPU peg just installed

Insert the second peg:

Second CPU peg going in

You should have a peg in both holes.

CPU peg, first one installed

Second CPU peg is installed

Our CPU has a logo side,

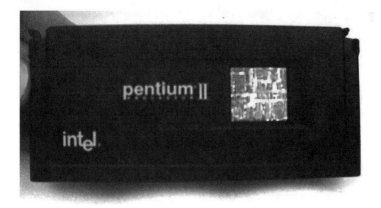

CPU, front view

and it has a fan/heatsink side:

CPU, fan view

Prepare the CPU by attaching the two fan mount brackets. Notice how each fan mount bracket has a clip at the bottom that locks onto the peg:

CPU fan mount, peg clip closed

Slide on each CPU fan mount bracket:

CPU fan clip, going on

CPU fan clip, just after being installed

Our CPU looks like this with the brackets:

CPU with both fan support clips installed

Install the CPU.

Place the CPU into the bracket on the motherboard.

CPU being plugged in

Push down until both clips on top of the CPU click in place. Lock both of the CPU fan clips onto the pegs. Next, we need to hook up the CPU fan power supply. Take the cord that looks like this:

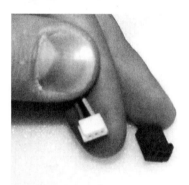

CPU fan connectors

Install the brown end on the motherboard. The connector is keyed to fit one way and is near the CPU.

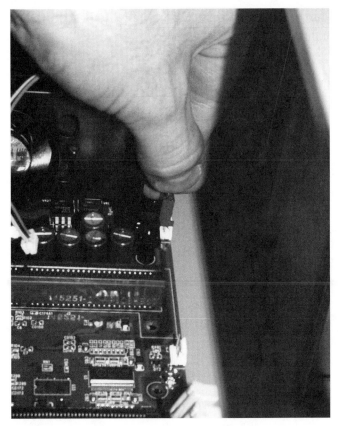

CPU fan power cord on motherboard side

Install the white end to the CPU fan. This connector is also keyed to fit one way.

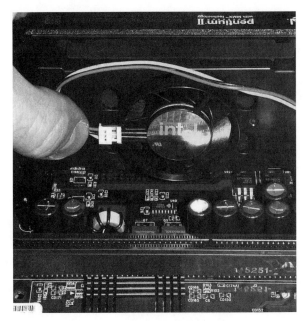

CPU fan power cord on CPU fan side

This fan is pretty cool! It is a variable RPM fan that is controlled by the temperature of the CPU. The hotter the CPU becomes, the faster the fan turns.

Installing the Motherboard

Place the motherboard into the case to check where you'll place the necessary standoffs.

Positioning the motherboard in the case

Take the motherboard back out, paying attention to holes in the motherboard that need a standoff. Our case needs two additional standoffs:

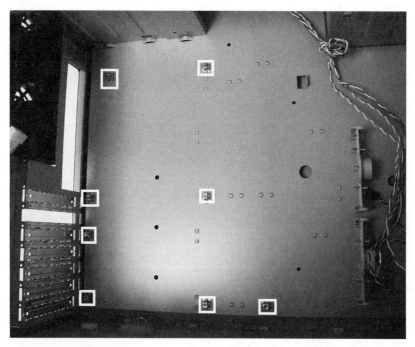

Case, standoffs marked

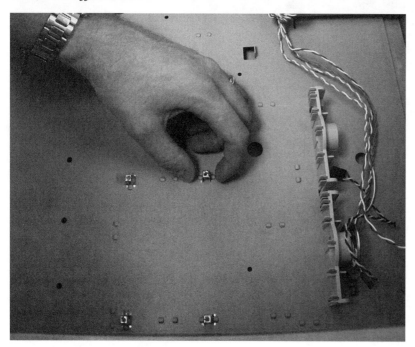

Case, first additional standoff

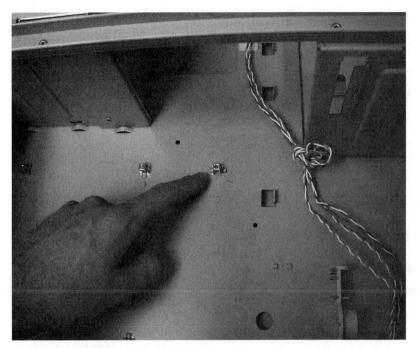

Case, second additional standoff

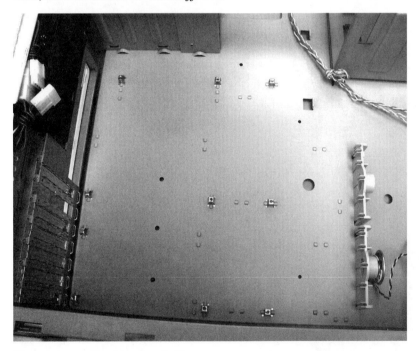

Empty case, showing standoffs

Now, place the motherboard in position, and fasten it using screws that are smooth under the head. Don't overtighten the screws. (Remember, start all the screws before tightening any.)

Motherboard, just placed in case

Next, let's provide power to the motherboard. Peek through the back of the case through the ATX opening. Find the ATX power connector on the motherboard. It's right next to the CPU.

ATX power supply on motherboard, side view

ATX power connector on motherboard

Attach the ATX power connector from the power supply. It only goes in one way, and has a clip to secure it in place.

ATX power connector being connected, top view

ATX motherboard connector, connected

Now we can go ahead and install the ATX backplate. Locate the plate and pop out the appropriate panels to allow the connectors to show through. Then, simply pop the plate into place.

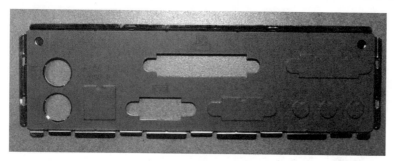

ATX plate, popouts in

ATX plate installed

Next, attach the accessory connectors. Here we hook up the power button, the reset button, the speaker, the hard drive activity LED and the power LED. Be sure to check the polarity by referring to the motherboard and case manuals. If you are unable to determine polarity for the LEDs, try each one. Reverse it if it doesn't light up. The polarity for the buttons doesn't matter. The polarity for the speaker is important, but if you can't figure it out, just try it, and if the speaker works, go with it.

Here's the pin diagram from our motherboard manual:

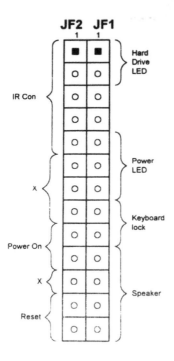

Switch connectors from manual

These connectors just push into place.

Reset Switch connector being attached

All connectors connected

Testing the redundant power supply

Now is a good time to test the redundant power supply. Attach both power supplies to a power source using separate power cords. Set both power switches to the on position. Push the power button on the front of the case. Once the server comes on, pull one (and only one) of the power cords. The server should stay on, and the buzzer should emit a loud warning sound. Once you have tested the power supply, unplug both of them and continue with assembly.

The Drives

Hard Drives

Look over the top and the bottom of each of the three hard drives:

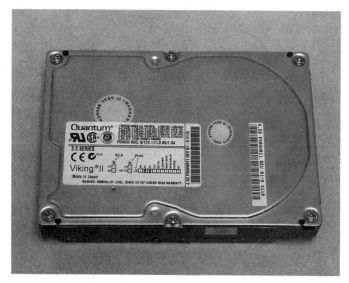

Hard drive on bench, top view

Hard drive on bench, bottom view

On our Quantum drives, notice all three locations for jumpers. On the bottom:

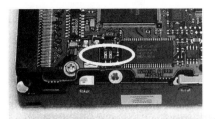

Bottom jumpers

Near the front (as seen from the bottom):

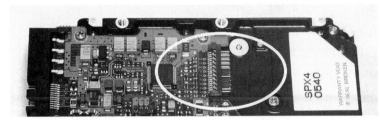

Front hard drive jumpers

And on the back (drive shown upside down for photographic purposes):

Hard drive on bench, rear view, jumpers marked

Also, notice the wide SCSI connector and the power connector on the back of the hard drive:

Hard drive on bench, rear view, wide SCSI connector marked

Hard drive on bench, rear view, power connector marked

The wide SCSI connector is shaped like a trapezoid so it only fits one way. The power connector is also keyed so it only goes in one way.

Normally, we would just hook up the SCSI connector and power, and then use jumpers to set the SCSI ID number and the termination. However, since this is a server, we want to be able to pull out the hard drives while the system is running. So, we will be installing the hard drives into cartridges which slide into frames that are permanently attached to the case.

The cartridge fits into the receiving frame, and then the keylock is turned to activate power to the drive.

Removable cartridge insert, closed up

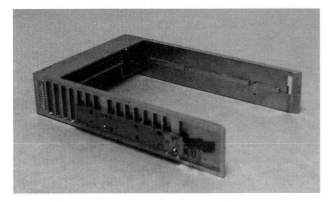

Removable hard drive bracket, on bench, side view, with rails installed

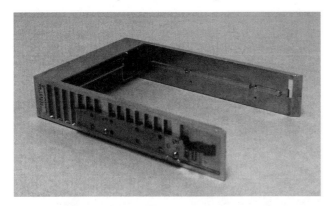

Removable Cartridge on bench with keys in lock

Open one of the removable cartridge inserts.

Cartridge cover coming off

Inside we find a bag of screws and some keys.

Removable cartridge, cover off, brand new

Remove the bottom in the same manner as the top. Notice we have a wide SCSI connector, a power connector and some jumper connectors.

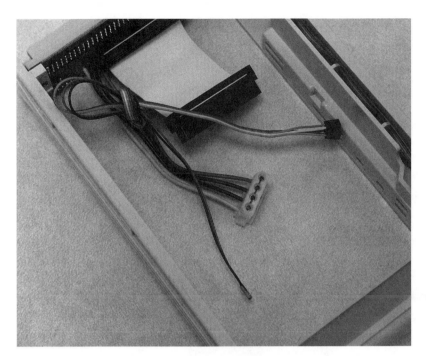

Removable cartridge, close up of connectors

NOTE: Before installing the hard drives, remove any and all termination and SCSI ID jumpers and discard them. We will use the wires inside the cartridge instead.

Attach the wide SCSI connector to the drive.

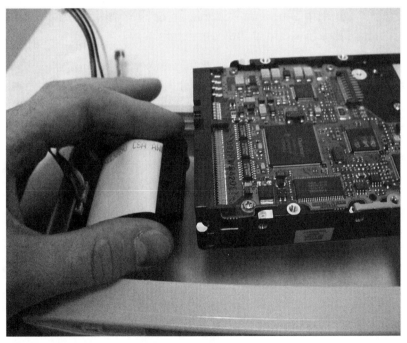

Attach ribbon cable to hard drive

Next, attach the power connector.

Attach power supply to hard drive

NOTE: This next part requires utmost care to avoid damaging the ribbon cable.

Ribbon cables do not flex from side to side. The only way to flex sideways is to bend the cable in the shape of a "Z" and carefully adjust the amount of cable on each portion of the bends. NEVER allow the cable to crease, pinch, or strain at the connectors.

Start by pre-bending the ribbon cable into a "Z" shape. Carefully adjust the amount of cable to allow the drive to sit in the proper position. Be sure the rest of the wires are out of the way.

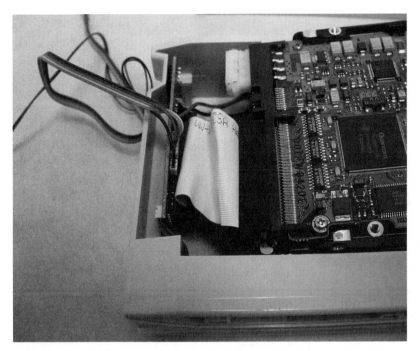

Ribbon cable with initial bends

Ease the ribbon cable into place, gently coaxing the ribbon cable as you go. Be certain there are no creases, pinches or strains on the cable.

Ease the hard drive into place. Now, attach the screws to secure the drive to the bracket.

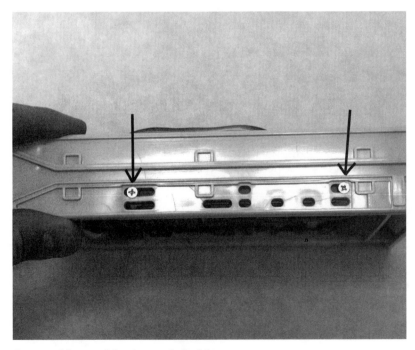

Removable cartridge insert, left-side screws

Removable cartridge insert, right-side screws

Now, feed the jumper wires around to the jumper pins. Going over the top and around the front seems to be the best route for the Quantum drives:

Removable cartridge, jumpers installed

NOTE: It is extremely important to consult the manuals for the drive bracket and the hard drive to be certain that you are installing the wires with the correct pins and the correct polarity.

Once you have installed the jumper wires, examine the ribbon cable to make sure it is properly in place and is not pinched, creased, or strained.

Ribbon cable, top view

Ribbon cable in removable cartridge

Perfect!

Now, put the covers back on.

Cartridge cover going back on

Repeat this process for the rest of the hard drives.

After all the drives are encased in enclosures, we need to set the hard drive SCSI ID. On the back of each enclosure, rotate the ID indicator using a small flathead screwdriver. Set each ID indicator to a different ID number. We have chosen "4," "5" and "6" for our hard drives. The RAID controller will use "7." Note that settings "A" through "F" represent 10-15 in hexadecimal.

Setting the SCSI ID on cartridges

Set the cartridges aside for now.

CD-ROM

First, we need to attach the rails to the drives with the small screws provided. Let's start with the CD-ROM drive.

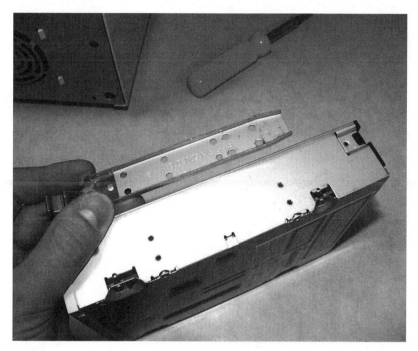

Rail about to be attached to CD-ROM drive

CD ROM, rail being attached

Test the CD-ROM drive's depth by inserting it into place, and then attach the case's front panel.

CD ROM drive being pushed in place to test depth

Make sure the CD ROM drive is flush with the front panel.

CD ROM drive, flush with panel

If necessary, adjust the mounting position of the rails on the drive by relocating them to the next set of holes.

Set aside the CD-ROM drive, and look at the rest of the drives. In a manner similar to the CD-ROM drive rails, install rails on the tape drive, the floppy drive, and each of the hard drive bracket receiving frames.

Floppy on bench

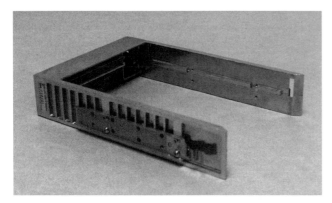

Removable hard drive bracket, on bench, side view, with rails installed

DDS drive on bench

Special Note

If you look closely at the Travan tape, you'll notice that it doesn't go in the drive all the way. If you have a Travan-style tape drive, mount the rails further forward, so that the drive will sit further back. This way, the tape won't stick out so far, and you can still close the front of the case!

TR-4 drive on bench

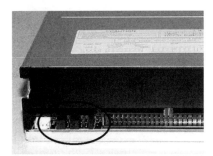

TR-4 tape being pulled out of drive, angle chosen to show depth

Next, we need to set the SCSI IDs and termination for the narrow SCSI devices (the tape and CD drive). Using jumpers, choose a device for the end of the chain. Install a jumper on the termination pins for the device on the end of the chain. (Only do this for one drive.) Next, select a unique ID for each drive, installing jumpers on each set of pins necessary to set the ID. (You may need to refer to the owner's manual for each device to verify the correct pins for each ID.)

We've set the CD-ROM drive to SCSI ID "3" with termination. The CD-drive will be the last device in the chain.

CD-ROM, rear view, jumpers marked

We've set the tape drive to SCSI ID "2" with no termination.

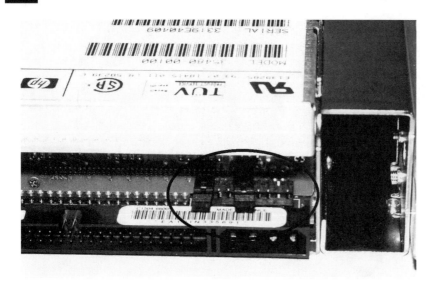

Tape drive, rear view, jumpers marked

After attaching all of the rails and setting SCSI IDs, slide the components into place, one at a time:

CD ROM being pushed in place to test depth

CD and tape drive in case

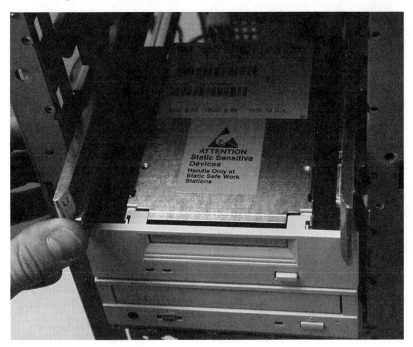

CD, tape, and one frame in case

CD, tape, and two frames in case

Slide all three of the frames as well as the CD drive and the tape drive into the case. Also, slide each removable hard drive cartridge into place and lock them in with the key.

Turning key on all hard drive cartridges

The Floppy Drive

Now, run the power cable and the ribbon cable for the floppy drive out the front of the case through the floppy drive bay. Attach the power connector and the ribbon cable. If your ribbon cable fits both ways, be sure the red-striped wire is nearest the pin marked "1" on the printed circuit board (this is usually closest to the power supply connector).

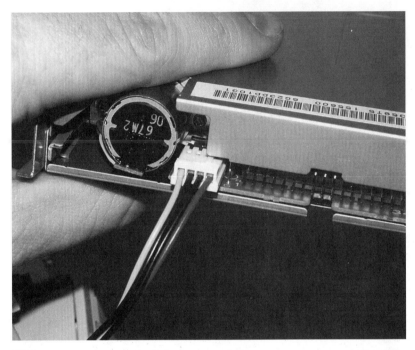

Floppy power connector being connected

Floppy drive connectors connected

Insert the floppy drive into the case until the rails snap into place.

From the side, the case should look like this:

All drives installed, side view, no cables yet

The Data Cables

Now we need to attach the data cables: two SCSI cables and a floppy cable. Attach one end of the Wide SCSI cable to an external terminator. These terminators cost about $25. This is necessary because during a failure, you might be removing the last hard drive. If you terminate that drive, then your termination is lost when you remove the drive. Using an external terminator, the chain is always terminated.

Terminator

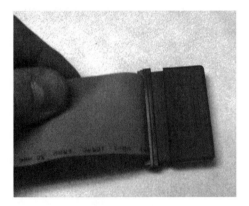

Terminator on end of cable

Attach each Wide SCSI device to any of the connectors in the center of the cable. Don't attach a device to the ends. Now, attach the free end of the cable to the motherboard.

Wide SCSI cable being installed

Next, do the same for the narrow SCSI cable, except you won't need a terminator if you have terminated the last device on the chain. Be sure to attach one end of the cable to a terminator or a terminated device! Your cables should look like this:

CD and Tape drive cables connected

Most of the data cables are in place, so let's attach the floppy cable to the motherboard as well:

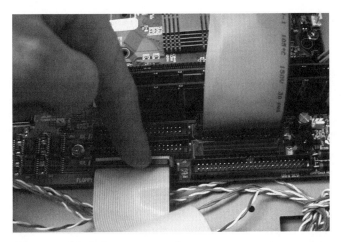

Floppy cable being connected

And, of course, attach the narrow SCSI cable to the motherboard.

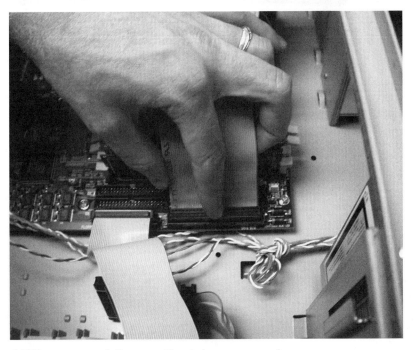

SCSI narrow and floppy cables being connected

Next, install a power connector to each device. It makes no difference which ones you use. When you're done, it should look like this:

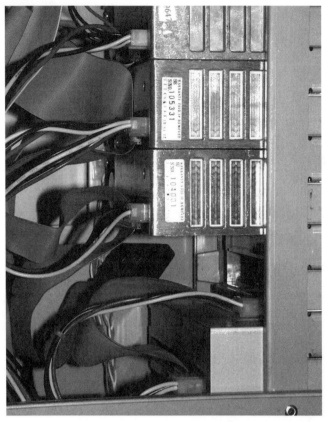

All power and SCSI connectors connected

The Cards

Examine each of the cards we will be installing. Our video card is the Matrox Mystique PCI:

This is the Adaptec RAIDport II RAID controller:

This is our Network Interface Card (NIC):

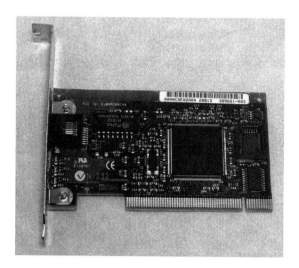

Your cards should appear similar to these.

Installing the Cards

Prepare the case by pushing out the appropriate slot covers in the case to accommodate the cards.

About to push out the slot cover plate

Let's start by installing the RAID controller. Just push it in, straight down, using even pressure to ensure you won't damage the card. Be sure to insert this card into the RAIDport II slot.

RAID card being pushed in

Do the same with the other cards. Be sure the cards don't contact each other. If you have the luxury of space, spread the cards out evenly among the available slots to allow more airflow in between them.

All cards installed

Insert a screw into the notch in each card and fasten them to the case with a screwdriver.

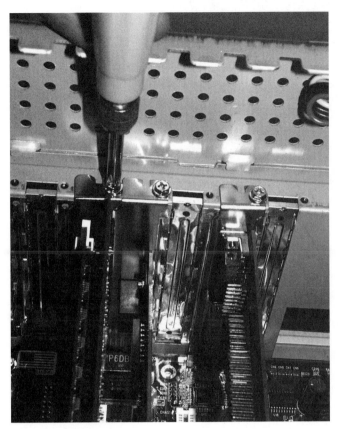

Screw in all cards

Final Touches

Once all the cards are installed, let's finish by attaching a power supply connector to each bank of fans.

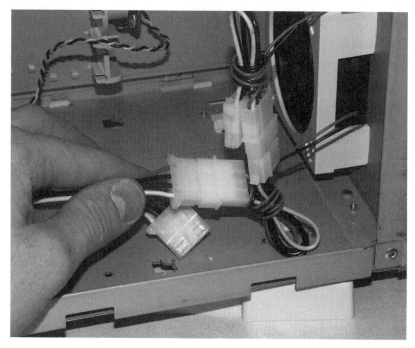

Front fan power supply being connected

Rear fan power being connected

Also, tie up any loose wiring to prevent it from interfering with fans. Use tie straps with tie downs and twist ties to make everything neat and tidy inside the case.

Extra cords wrapped up with twist ties

The Logo

Now, for the most important part; a server just isn't finished until we complete this step: Installation of the "Intel inside" sticker!

Find a good place on the case to display the sticker. We chose the lower-left corner.

Bare front corner of case

Front corner of case with logo

Hooking up Everything and a Clean Slate

Now, attach both power cords to the power supply, and plug both of them into the UPS. Attach the video cable from the monitor to the video card, and plug the monitor's power cord into the UPS. Attach your keyboard and mouse. Also, attach the serial cable from the UPS to one of the server's serial ports. Attach the serial cable from the external modem to the server's other serial port. Plug the power supply for the modem into the UPS as well. Don't attach the network connector until your server is configured.

A clean slate

Our server is fully assembled and is ready to be configured. It's a clean slate, ready to be put to work.

Let's move on to configuration and software installation!

Chapter 5:
Installing Windows NT Server

This book, including this chapter, focuses on the hardware aspects of setting up a Windows NT server. Aspects not affecting the hardware are addressed, but you may wish to have a book on Windows NT Administration available for reference during this phase of building your server.

First Starting Up

When you first turn on the computer, you will see a splash screen from the video card:

Video BIOS startup screen

This shows for just a moment, then you'll see the main BIOS startup screen:

First BIOS startup screen

For our BIOS, pressing the ⌊Del⌋ key will open the BIOS setup program:

After pressing the [Delete] *key*

Configuring the BIOS settings

Every BIOS has several settings, and it seems every computer has different options for these settings. All settings fall into two categories: options that affect whether or not components of the system will function, and those that affect how well the system functions. For example, the BIOS setup may allow a user to enable or disable the integrated SCSI controller. Turning this off renders the SCSI system useless. However, the setup may also allow the user to disable ECC on the Level II cache of the CPU. As we discussed in Chapter Three, ECC is important, but the system may function its entire life without any noticeable difference if you turn it off.

As you go through the menus, pay attention to the settings in the BIOS setup. Experiment with different settings before bringing the system online. If you are unsure of any particular setting, choose the default, then spend some time researching the implications of a different setting before changing it. Remember, this is a server; it's important to keep it running even if all settings are not optimal.

Here are a couple resources for BIOS settings and their implications. First and foremost is the motherboard's owner's manual. Also visit their Website. The company that wrote the actual BIOS software may also have tips on its Website. If you are unsuccessful, try some books and other Websites. Tom's Hardware Guide is by far the coolest Website for hardware (www.tomshardware.com). Also, Tom has a new book out by the same name. Also available is *The BIOS Companion*. This book contains nothing but BIOS information. A new edition is due soon. Experience will teach you a lot as well. As always, change one thing at a time; if a particular setting causes a problem, change it back!

Our BIOS setup program offers quite a few options. Let's go through just a few of the screens. Remember, your BIOS setup screens may look nothing like these. Here's the main startup screen:

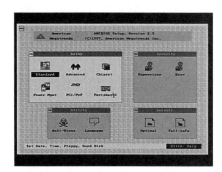

BIOS main screen

Under "Advanced Setup," choose the boot order of devices. List the floppy first and then the SCSI bus. Don't list the IDE.

BIOS setup boot SCSI

Under "Chipset Setup," go to *DRAM integrity mode* and select *ECC Hardware*. This will allow the chipset to correct for one-bit memory errors.

DRAM ECC mode screen

Under "Advanced Setup," select *CPU ECC* and choose *Enabled*. This allows the L-II cache to also use ECC. (You must have a Pentium II 300 or higher or the ECC version of a Pentium II 266 to use this option.)

CPU ECC enabled screen

Next, go to "Peripheral Setup" and choose *Onboard IDE* and set it to *Disabled*.

IDE disabled screen

Also under "Peripheral Setup," look at the CPU overheat warning buzzer temperature. Here you can see the actual current temperature as well as the threshold at which the buzzer will sound. We're leaving ours at the default, 55° Celsius.

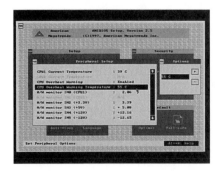

CPU overheat temp BIOS screen

When you're through choosing your initial BIOS settings, just click on the upper left corner and click on "Save changes and Exit."

BIOS exit screen

Configuring the RAID Controller

Settings for the SCSI controller

First thing we need to do to configure the RAID is to configure the SCSI settings. As the computer boots, press Ctrl+A when prompted by the "Press Ctrl+A for SCSI Select Utility" message.

Boot Screen

The system enters the SCSI Select main screen. The utility first prompts you to select a channel to configure. Let's start with channel "A."

Channel A in SCSI Select

Next, we choose to Configure or View settings or run the SCSI disk utility. Choose the first option, "Configure/ View Host Adapter Settings."

Configure, View settings on Channel A

The screen for basic configuration appears.

Configuration main sub screen, Channel A

Set all options to *Enabled* and put the Host Adapter to ID 7. Next, choose to enter the Advanced options.

Under Additional Options, there's a SCSI Device Configuration option which goes to this screen:

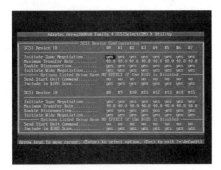

SCSI Device Configuration Page

Settings for individual devices can be set here. You shouldn't need to set any of these options unless you are having problems. If your tape drive or CD-ROM drive isn't working, try slowing down the maximum transfer rate or turning off the "Initiate Wide Negotiation" option.

When you're done, press Esc, and you'll be given the chance to save. Choose *Yes* to save the changes.

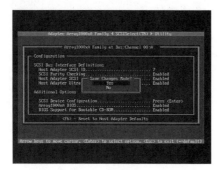

Save changes to SCSI Select Channel A

This takes us back to the SCSI Select introduction screen, where we can Configure or View our settings for channel B. We repeat the process for Channel B and save any changes.

To see what devices are on a particular channel, choose that channel, then select "SCSI Disk Utilities."

SCSI Disk Utilities on Channel A

The next screen will show what devices are on what channels.

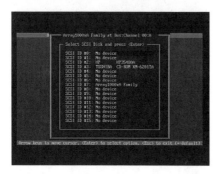

SCSI Disk Utilities main screen, Channel A

We can do the same for channel B:

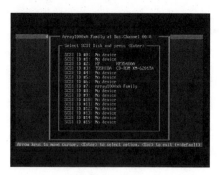

SCSI Disk Utilities main screen, channel B

This is useful if we forget which devices have which SCSI IDs.

When you're all done, press (Esc) at the channel selection screen, and answer *Yes* to the prompt to exit.

Exit SCSI Select Utility

Then hit any key to reboot.

Now, when our server reboots, all devices should show up in the SCSI bus scan:

Booting up, full main BIOS

The boot up will fail because it can't find the Operating System. First, we need to create an array.

Flashing the RAID Controller BIOS

Our Adaptec ARO-1130SA RAID controller card comes with two books, one about the card and one about the included software. The books are excellent resources and make the configuration very easy. Our RAID controller comes with four diskettes.

The first step is to boot the BIOS and Driver Selection Utility diskette.

BIOS and driver selection utility main screen

This utility examines our system and then flashes the RAID controller's BIOS.

Updating BIOS

The utility then informs us which of the two driver diskettes to use, Disk A or Disk B. Our system told us to use Disk A. Then we press any key to reboot.

Driver Update, press any key to reboot

Creating an Array

Next, boot the ArrayConfigSA diskette.

Booting the ArrayConfig Floppy

From the main menu, select "Disk Array Operations."

ArrayConfigSA main menu, select Disk Array Operations

The Disk Array main sub menu will come up. Choose "Create New Array."

Disk Array main sub menu, Create new array option selected

We need to select the type of array we want to create. Select RAID 5.

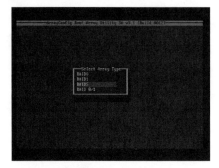

Selecting RAID level 5

Now, we need to name the array. For simplicity, let's call it "array1."

Type in an array name

Typed in array1 for the name

Input the number of hard drives to be used for the array (excluding hot spares). For our server, that's "3."

How many drives will your array have?

Next, we choose which hard drives to include. We're going to include all of them.

Include the first drive in RAID 5 array

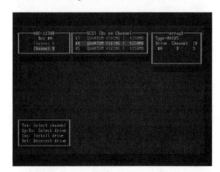

Include the second drive in RAID 5 array

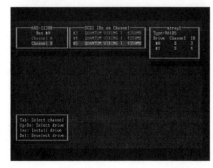

Include the third drive in RAID 5 array

Next, we need to format the array. Here we have the choice of low-level formatting or initializing the array with zeroes.

Initialize Array to Zero option

Choose to initialize the array with zeroes. Low-level formatting is not necessary.

The software gives you a choice of data block sizes. If your server will be used for both large and small files, or if you don't know, choose the 64K block size.

64K block size option

Go ahead and initialize the array. (Note: This can take a *long* time. It may take over an hour for this to complete.)

Writing zeros to array, 25 pct complete

Writing zeros to array, 100 pct complete

Initialization of Array1 complete

Press ⌜Escape⌝ to return to the main menu. Choose to "Display Boot Order."

Main menu ArconfigSA

The boot order will be listed. Since we only have one array, it should be selected as the boot array.

Boot order selection

Press ⟨Esc⟩ all the way back to the main menu and then exit. The software prompts us "Do you want to exit ARConfig and reboot?"

Exit ArrayConfigSA and reboot

To which we answer *Yes*.

The array is now a device. It will interact with the Operating System as a single device.

Installing Windows NT

Initial Setup (Text-based Setup)

Fortunately, Windows NT CDs are bootable and so is our CD-ROM drive (and our drive controller). Put the Windows NT Server CD in the CD-ROM drive and boot the CD-ROM.

BIOS with bootable CD in drive

When the screen says, "Setup is examining your computer's hardware configuration…" press the F6 key. (If you miss it, setup will abort. Just reboot again.)

Setup is inspecting your computer's hardware configuration

Setup will pause, and the following screen comes up:

After pressing F6

5 Installing Windows NT Server 4.0

Press ⑤ to add an additional driver to Windows NT setup.

Choose "Other" for type of Mass driver

Choose "Other" and press ⏎.

Next, insert the correct driver diskette (in our case, diskette A) and press ⏎ Enter.

Insert disk for Mass storage driver.

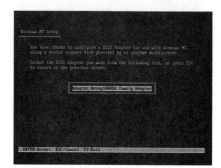

Use this driver

Confirming inclusion of mass storage driver

Press ⏎Enter to accept the drivers (note that the "Adaptec Array1000xA Family Adapter" is now listed and will be loaded).

NT setup will continue and stop at the Welcome screen. Press ⏎Enter to continue.

Welcome to setup

Setup will list the RAID controller driver and ask if we want to add any more. We don't, so press ⏎Enter to continue.

listing all main drivers

Setup alerts you that the disk contains more than 1024 cylinders and won't work properly in MS-DOS. That's just fine, since we are installing Windows NT Server 4.0. Press ⏎Enter to continue.

Disk has more than 1024 cylinders

Setup notices that the disk array is completely blank or contains an OS that cannot coexist with Windows NT. Since our disk array is indeed blank, press Ⓒ to continue.

Disk must be new

Read through the License Agreement, and press ⌨F8 when you get to the bottom.

License agreement, top

License agreement, bottom

Setup stops to confirm that it has chosen the correct base hardware. Press ⌈Enter⌉ to continue.

The above list matches my computer

Next, setup lists the available partitions on which to install Windows NT. Since none exists, it lists only the unpartitioned space.

Choose a partition

Normally, we would install Windows NT in the unpartitioned space, and it would partition and format automatically. However, Windows NT contains a bug and a limitation. The limitation is that it cannot boot a partition larger than 7.8 GB on a SCSI disk. The bug is that Windows NT Setup cannot format a partition larger than 4 GB. Since our drive is larger than 7.8 GB, we will have to have more than one partition. (If you want a boot partition that is larger than 4 GB, consult article ID Q119497 in the Microsoft Knowledge Base.)

163

Our server has about 9 GB of usable space. This means we must have more than one partition anyway, so we have chosen to create three partitions. The first partition will be 2 GB. The last partition is going to be used just for swapping, so we allocated about 700 MB that we will use just for the swap file. The middle partition contains everything else, and in our case is 6 GB. All partitions are NTFS. Don't use FAT. FAT is only useful on a workstation where you boot NT and Win95 on the same partition. NTFS is a superior file system. Also, Windows NT version 4.0 cannot read or boot FAT32. Use NTFS.

Press C to create a partition. Indicate a size of 2 GB.

Setup returns to the previous menu, this time listing the 2 GB partition. Select it and press Enter.

Selecting new partition

Next, we need to format the partition.

Select to format NTFS

Setup prompts us with the default directory to install NT. Choose \WINNT for installation.

Install to the WINNT directory.

Setup then examines the disk, and in our case, finds nothing.

Setup examines your disks

Setup then copies files to the hard drive.

Setup copies files to hard drive.

When Setup is finished, it prompts you to remove the CD or floppy, then press any key to reboot.

Setup is done, so reboot.

The computer reboots, and the NT kernel loads.

NT booting the kernel.

The startup process pauses while the boot partition is converted to NTFS.

NT converting to NTFS

Final Setup (Graphical)

When the initial text-based setup is completed and the conversion is done, the system will restart and boots into the graphical portion of Windows NT setup. Refer to the Installation portion of the Microsoft Windows NT Server manual for more details on the final installation steps while we briefly cover a few of the options here.

TIP: As you go through the installation, install any options you think you might want, including drivers, protocols and services. At the end of the installation process, you'll want to run Service Pack 4. However, if you install any components after running the service pack, you have to run the service pack again. But, you can remove components you don't want after running the service pack without penalty.

NOTE: You will be given the option to assign this computer to be a Domain Controller. If you do not assign it to be a Domain Controller during installation, you will not have the chance later. The only way to make a Windows NT server a Domain Controller is to pick that option during installation. How do you know if you will want it to be a Domain Controller? If you are going to have more than one server in your network, consider having a domain. If you have a domain, you will need a Primary Domain Controller. Learn more about Windows NT domains in any book about Windows NT administration.

The first things you'll need to enter are you're name and organization. Since people come and go from companies, it's more practical to enter something like "Network Administrator" or some other title for the name. Then enter your company name for the organization.

When prompted for the CD-Key number, you'll find the information imprinted on a sticker that's normally found on the back of the CD jewel case.

For Licensing Modes, you have two choices: "Per Server" requires us to buy one license for every concurrent connection made by a client to this server. "Per Seat" requires us to buy a license for every computer that accesses Windows NT Server. Microsoft allows a one-time change in an organization;s licensing structure from "Per Server" to "Per Seat." You can use the "License Manager" control panel to do this at a later date. However, you cannot legally change your licensing structure back to "Per Server" after you have changed it to "Per Seat."

Your computer will also need a name. The three most common names for a group of three servers are Larry, Curly and moe in a domain called "Stooge." Also common are Homer, Marge, Lisa, Bart and Maggie in a domain called "Springfield." Still others like to name their servers after Greek Gods. At Calvin College, in Grand Rapids, Michigan, all Unix servers have names starting with "U," all Novell servers have a name starting with "L", and all NT servers have a name starting with "N." Some organizations that are spread out like to name their servers with the name of the city they are in. Some companies seem to squelch creativity and simply name servers things like "server1" and "server2." We chose a name for our server which is appropriate for our organization. Our server's name is "Dusty."

You'll need to specify whether or not this server will be a Domain Controller. Warning: If you select "Stand Alone Server," it is impossible to change it to be a Domain Controller. Backup Domain Controllers can be promoted to Primary, but Stand Alone servers remain Stand Alone servers forever. For that reason, we suggest you select "Primary Domain Controller."

When prompted to enter the Administrator Account password, this should be totally obscure. The best way to choose the Administrator password is randomly. Random character generators work well, but usually are too hard to remember, and end up being written on a sticky note and stuck to the monitor for all to see. Instead, try an acronym (the first letter of every word) formed by a phrase that's easy to remember. However, don't use a cliché. That's too easy. Another good way is to open a dictionary or phone book and randomly point to a spot on the page. Use whatever word you are pointing at combined with some punctuation and some numbers.

Be sure to create an Emergency Repair Disk when asked. Say Yes and insert a blank floppy disk into the drive. Put this floppy in a safe and secure place after it's created; if someone else gets ahold of it, they may be able to gain access to the server!

Choose everything when you get the option to select what components are to be installed. Later, it's easy to delete stuff you don't need, but it's more difficult to add.

When the networking support is installed, you may have to instruct NT to install the drivers from the manufacturer supplied diskette. Then install the desired protocols and/or services for your particular networking environment, and pick an appropriate domain name.

Near the end of the setup process, install the ODBC SQL Server Driver and choose the appropriate Time Zone for your location. Setup will then find a VGA-compatible display adapter. Don't change this now; change this after you reboot. Remember, video drivers must be completely compatible with the system and should be certified by Microsoft. If you experience any problems, use the default VGA adapter. When setup is done, click the button to restart the computer.

Booting for the First Time

After the computer restarts, the main startup window will appear. Press Ctrl + Alt + Del to log on. When the logon screen comes up, enter the Administrator Password and click OK. Click the Close button when the first "Tip of the Day" appears and we're ready to finish setting up the hard drive.

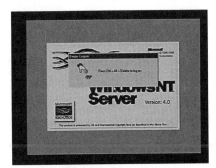

Press Ctrl + Alt + Del to log on

The logon screen comes up. Enter the Administrator Password and click OK.

Logon Information

The first "Tip of the Day" comes up. Click Close.

Did you know...

The first thing we need to do is add two more partitions to the hard drive. Let's make a partition for data and a partition dedicated to the swap file. Start by opening the Disk Administrator. Go to the [Start] menu and click **Programs | Administrative Tools (Common) | Disk Administrator**. The Disk Administrator will load.

[Start] *Programs | Administrative Tools | Disk Administrator*

Disk Administrator screen

Right-click in the free space and choose "Create."

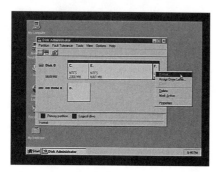

Disk Administrator warns us that MS-DOS won't be able to read a disk with more than one primary partition. Click [Yes].

Not MS-DOS

Input a size for the data partition. For us, 6000 MB will leave us a hefty size partition to be used for swap of about 700 MB.

Create size; click $\boxed{OK}$

Repeat the process for the swap partition. Use the remaining hard drive space, about 700 MB.

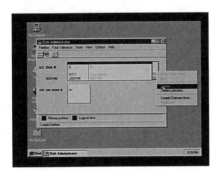

Right-click Create Swap Partition

No MS-DOS #2

Specify swap partition size

No MS-DOS #3

When finished creating the partitions, right-click in the newly formed partition and choose "Commit changes now…" Click Yes at the confirmation.

Right-click; commit changes now #2

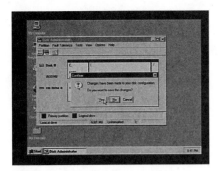

DA commit changes now #2

Click [OK]; remember to make a new RDISK later.

Rdisk OK #2

Now we must format the partitions. Right-click and choose format.

Right-click; format E

Choose NTFS from the Combo Box.

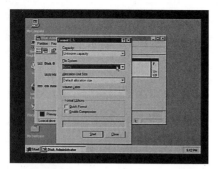

Choose NTFS

Click ⌊Start⌋ to begin formatting. Click ⌊OK⌋ to confirm.

Format window click ⌊Start⌋

Click ⌊OK⌋ at the format warning

When the formatting is done, click ⌊OK⌋. Click ⌊Close⌋ on the format window.

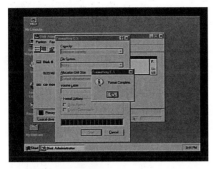

Format complete!

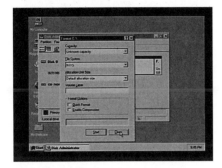

Format Close

Exit the Disk Administrator.

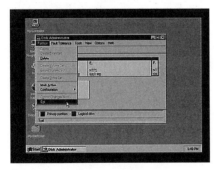

Exit Disk Administrator

Now we will assign the swap file to our dedicated partition. Right-click My Computer. Select **Properties**.

Right-Click Opening My Computer's Properties

Click on the *Performance* tab.

The Performance tab

Click on the Change button for Virtual Memory.

Change Virtual Memory

Click on the F drive, and then set the Virtual Memory size to almost all of the partition size, then click Set.

Click on F

Click on the C drive, and reduce the size to 2 MB (the minimum size allowed), and click ⌈Set⌉.

Click on C drive

Click ⌈OK⌉ to confirm.

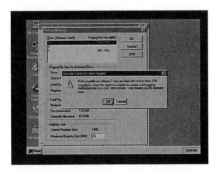

No debugging

Click ⌈OK⌉ to close the Virtual Memory window, and click ⌈Close⌉ on the System Properties window.

Virtual memory click O.K.

Close System Properties

Click [Yes] to restart.

Restart after changing virtual memory.

After the system reboots, logon and open the control panels. Double-click on Tape Devices.

Tape Devices

Click the [Detect] button, then click [OK] when NT finds the tape drive.

Tape drive found

Place the Windows NT CD in the CD drive in order to add the drivers.

Place NT CD in the drive.

Click [OK] once the driver is loaded.

Click [OK] after tape driver is added

That's it! Our Windows NT Server is now ready for action. From here, start learning Windows NT Administration from whatever source you choose. Consider becoming certified by Microsoft. A final warning: whatever you do, be sure your system is secure before bringing it into service.

Good luck and happy computing!

Shopping List: This shopping list will help you organize the features that you want for each of the major components you want in your system. You can make additional copies of this checklist.

	Manufacturer #1	Cost	Comments	Manufacturer #2	Cost	Comments
Case						
CD-ROM drive						
Data Cables						
Drive Controllers						
Fans						
Floppy Drive						
Hard Drive #1						
Hard Drive #2						
Hubs						
ISDN Adapter						
Keyboard/Mouse						
KVM (Keyboard/Video/Mouse) Switch Boxes						
Modem						
Monitor						
Motherboard						
Network cabling						
Network Interface Card (NIC)						
Operating systemn (OS)						
Power Supply						
Processor						
RAID controller						
RAM						
Routers						
Servers						
Switches						
Tape Drives						
Uninterruptible Power Supply/Source (UPS)						
Video card